An Introduction to

Company Law

in the Commonwealth Caribbean

This publication was sponsored and facilitated by
Institute of Chartered Accountants of the Caribbean (ICAC)

An Introduction to

Company Law

in the Commonwealth Caribbean

Rambarran MANGAL

Canoe Press

University of the West Indies

● Barbados ● Jamaica ● Trinidad and Tobago

Canoe Press
University of the West Indies
1A Aqueduct Flats, Kingston 7, Jamaica, W I

Cataloguing in Publication Data

Mangal, Rambarran
   Introduction to company law in the Commonwealth
   Caribbean / Rambarran Mangal.

   p. cm.
   ISBN: 978-976-8125-21-7
   Includes bibliographical references.
   1. Corporation law – Caribbean,
   English-speaking. I. Title.
   II. Title : Company law.
   KGJ328.M36 1995   346.066 dc-20

Book design by Prodesign Ltd., Kingston, Jamaica
Composed in Times and Gill Sans
in Ventura Publisher 4.1

Table of Contents

Foreword   *vii*

Preface   *viii*

Table of Cases   *ix*

Sources   *xiii*

Regional Legislation   *xiv*

United Kingdom Acts   *xv*

Chapter 1   Introduction   *1*

Chapter 2   Legal Forms of Business   *10*

Chapter 3   Characteristics of a Registered Company   *14*

Chapter 4   Incorporation   *21*

Chapter 5   The Memorandum of Association   *32*

Chapter 6   The Articles of Association   *49*

Chapter 7   Promotion of Companies   *72*

Chapter 8   The Rule in Turquand's Case   *78*

Chapter 9   The Raising of Capital   *81*

Chapter 10   Maintenance of Capital   *100*

Chapter 11   Loan Capital   *107*

Chapter 12   Receivers and Managers   *113*

Chapter 13   Dividends   *116*

Chapter 14   Membership   *121*

Chapter 15   Meetings   *128*

Chapter 16	Majority Rule and Minority Protection	*145*
Chapter 17	Management and Control	*157*
Chapter 18	Auditors	*176*
Chapter 19	Accounts and Audit	*182*
Chapter 20	Reconstruction, Mergers, Takeovers and Arrangements	*210*
Chapter 21	Insider Dealing or Trading	*213*
Chapter 22	Winding-Up	*216*
Chapter 23	External Companies	*231*
Chapter 24	Administration and Supervision	*236*
Index		*239*

Foreword

The need for this kind of material had been advocated for many years as professionals of the Region recognized the need for students and practitioners to have literature on indigenous laws available to them.

The Institute of Chartered Accountants of the Caribbean (ICAC), being established since October 1988, sought, as one of its first goals, to commence the production of such literature. This book is the first of many and we are, indeed, indebted to the author, Mr Rambarran Mangal, as well as the dedicated team of persons who cooperated in making this book possible.

Recognition should therefore be given to Mrs Velma Newton, Chairman of the Company Law Text Committee (Barbados), Mr Patrick Toppin (Barbados), Mr L. Christopher Ram (Guyana) first Executive/Research Director of the ICAC, and Chairman of ICAC's Education and Examinations Committee. The Presidents and Committee Chairpersons of the respective institutes of the Region who provided technical data and copies of the laws of their countries are also in our debt.

This is the beginning of a series of professional and academic publications intended to assist in educating students for examinations as well as to provide reference for practitioners. It is, therefore, foundational in nature and being unique, as it spans the laws of some eight countries, will be subject to continuous review and update.

As the founding President of the ICAC, I hereby recommend this book to a broad cross-section of users.

Aulous F. Madden
President
Institute of Chartered Accountants of the Caribbean

Preface

The aim of this book is to give an elementary account of the law as applied to companies registered under the various Companies Acts within the Commonwealth Caribbean Region (CARICOM Region).

The book is intended for those studying Company Law in the Region. It has been designed to cover the Institute of Chartered Accountants of the Caribbean (ICAC) examination in Company Law but it is hoped that it can also be used by lawyers, accountants and other professionals.

Much of the reform in recent years in Company Law in the Region has been as a result of the report of the Working Party on the Harmonisation of Company Law in the Caribbean Community, published in 1979.

I would like to express my thanks to Ms Yvonne Khadian, of the firm of Aulous F. Madden & Company, Chartered Accountants, for deciphering my handwritten manuscript and producing the type-written text for publication. Also to Mrs Gloria Hamilton for reading through the text and making useful corrections.

R Mangal

Table of Cases

A & B C Chewing Gum Ltd [1975] 1 ALLER 1017

Allen v Gold Reefs of West Africa Ltd [1900] 1 Ch 656

Ashbury Railway Carriage & Iron Co v Riche [1875] 33 LT 450

Atwool v Merryweather [1868] 37 LJ Ch 35

Baillie v Oriental Telephone Co [1915] 1 Ch 503

Bamford v Bamford [1970] Ch 212

Barnett Hoares & Co v South London Tramways [1887] 18 QBD 815

Barron v Potter [1914] 1 Ch 895

Bell Houses Ltd v City Wall Properties Ltd [1966] 2 Q13 656

Boardman v Phipps [1967] 2 AC 46

Borland's Trustee v Steel Bros & Co Ltd [1901] 1 Ch 279

Bushell v Faith [1970] AC 1099

Cane v Jones [1980] 1 WLR 1451

Carruth v Imperial Chemical Industries [1937] AC 707

Centrebind Ltd [1966] 3 ALLER 889

City Equitable Fire Insurance Co Ltd [1925] Ch 407

Clemens v Clemens Bros Ltd [1976] 2 ALLER 268

Cotman v Brougham (1918) AC 514

Cranleigh Precision Engineering Ltd v Bryant [1964]

Customs & Excise Commissioners v Hedon Alpha Ltd [1981] 2
    ALLER 697

D P P v Kent & Sussex Contractors Ltd [1944] KB146

Dafen Tinplate Co Ltd v Llanelly Steel Co (1907) Ltd [1920] 2 Ch 124

Daimler Co Ltd v Continental Tyre & Rubber Co (GB) Ltd. [1916] 2 AC 307

Daniels v Daniels [1978] Ch 406

Dawson v African Consolidated Land & Trading Co [1898] 1 Ch 6

Dimbula Valley (Ceylon) Tea Co Ltd v Laurie [1961] Ch 353

Duomatic Ltd Re [1969] 2 Ch 365

Eley v Positive Govt Security Life Assurance Co Ltd [1876] 45 LJ 2B 451

Ebrahimi v Westbourne Galleries Ltd [1973] AC 360

Erlanger v New Sombrero Phosphate Co [1878] 3 App Cases 1218

Ewing v Buttercup Margarine Co Ltd [1917] 2 Ch 1

Exxon Corporation v Exxon Insurance Consultants International Ltd [1981] 3 WLR 541

Foss v Harbottle [1843] 2 Ha 461

Freeman & Lockyer v Buckhurst Park Properties (Mangal) Ltd [1964] 2 QB 480

Re German Date Coffee Co [1882] 20 Ch D 169

Gluckstein v Barnes [1900] AC 240

Greenhalgh v Arderne Cinemas [1951] Ch 286

H. L. Bolton (Engineering) Co Ltd v T. J. Grahan & Sons [1957] 1QB 159

Hartley Baird Ltd [1955] Ch 143

Hedley Byrne & Co Ltd v Heller & Partners [1964] AC 465

Hely-Hutchinson v Brayhead Ltd [1968] 12B 549

Hogg v Cramphorn Ltd [1967] Ch 254

Holmes v Keyes [1959] Ch 199

Horsley & Weight Ltd [1982] Ch 442

Howard v Patent Ivory Manufacturing Co [1888] 38 Ch D 156

Howard Smith Ltd v Ampol Petroleum Ltd [1974] AC 821

Industrial Development Consultants Ltd v Cooley [1972] 1 WLR 443

Introductions Ltd v National Provincial Bank [1970] Ch 199

J E B Fasteners Ltd v Marks, Bloom & Co [1983] 1 ALLER 583

Jones v Lipman [1962]1 ALLER 442

John Shaw & Sons (Salford) Ltd v Shaw [1935]

Kelner v Baxter [1866] LR 2 CP 174

Re Kingston Cotton Mill Co Ltd [1896] 2 Ch 279

Lagunas Nitrate Co v Lagunas Syndicate [1899] 2 Ch 392

Langer United Rubber Estates Ltd v Cradock (No 3) [1968]

Lee v Lee's Air Farming Ltd [1961] AC 12

Lennard's Carrying Co Ltd v Asiatic Petroleum Co Ltd [1915] AC 705

Levy v Abercorris Slate & Slab Co [1887] 37 Ch D 260

Lister v Romford Ice & Cold Storage Co Ltd [1957]

Littlewood's Mail Order Stores Ltd v IRC [1969]

Macaura v Northern Assurance Co Ltd [1925] AC 619

Menier v Hooper's Telegraph Works [1874] 9 Ch App 350

Moore v Bresler Ltd [1944]

Moorgate Mercantile Holdings Ltd [1980] 1 WLR 227

Natal Land & Colonisation Co Ltd v Pauline Colliery & Dev Syn Ltd [1904] AC 120

Newborne v Sensolid (Great Britain) Ltd [1954] 12B 45

Northumberland Avenue Hotel Co [1886] 33 Ch D 16

Ooregum Gold Mining Co of India v Roper [1892] AC 125

Panorama Developments Guildford Ltd v Fidelis Furnishing Fabrics Ltd [1971] 2 QB 711

Parke v Daily News Ltd [1962] Ch 927

Pavlides v Jensen [1956] Ch 565

Pender v Lushington [1877] 6 Ch D 70

Percival v Wright [1902] 2 Ch 421

Phonogram v Lane [1982] QB 938

Ramsgate Victoria Hotel Co Ltd v Montefiore [1866] LR 1 Ex 109

Read v Astoria Garage (Streatham) Ltd [1952] Ch 637

Regal (Hastings) Ltd v Gulliver [1942] 1 ALLER 378

Rights & Issues Investment Trust Ltd v Stylo Shoes Ltd [1965] Ch 250

Rolled Steel Products Ltd v British Steel Corporation [1985] Ch 246

Royal British Bank v Turquand [1856] 6 E&B 327

Salomon v Salomon & Company [1897] AC 22

Scottish Insurance Corporation Ltd v Wilsons & Clyde Coal Co Ltd [1949] AC 462

Seibe Gorman & Co Ltd v Barclays Bank Ltd [1979]

Sharp v Dawes [1876] 2 BD 26

Sidebottom v Kershaw, Leese & Co Ltd [1920] 1 Ch 154

Smith, Stone & Knight Ltd v Birmingham Corp [1939] 4 ALLER 116

Southern Foundries (1926) Ltd v Shirlaw [1940] AC 701

Tesco Supermarkets Ltd v Nattrass [1972] AC 153

Thomas Marshall (Exports) v Guinle [1979] Ch 227

Re Thomas Gerrard & Sons Ltd [1968] Ch 455

Torquay Hotel Co v Cousins [1969]

Trevor v Whitworth [1887] 12 App Cas 409

Twycross v Grant [1877] 2 CPD 469

Unit Construction Co Ltd v Bullock [1960] AC 351

Wallersteiner v Moir [1975] QB 373

White v Bristol Aeroplane Co Ltd [1953] Ch 65

Wood v Odessa Waterworks Co [1889] 42 Ch D 636

Re Yenidje Tobacco Co Ltd [1916] 2 Ch 426

Yorkshire Woolcombers Assoc Ltd [1903] 2 Ch 284

Sources

Texts

1. *Report of the Working Party on the Harmonisation of Company Law in the Caribbean Community* (1979)

2. *Pennington's Company Law* – 5th Edition – Butterworths (1985)

3. *The Principles of Modern Company Law* by L. C. B. Gower, 2nd Edition – Stevens & Sons Ltd. (1957)

4. *Charlesworth and Morse Company Law* – 14th Edition – Geoffrey Morse (Sweet & Maxwell) (1991)

5. Company Law by K. R. Abbott – 4th Edition – D P Publications Ltd. (1990)

6. *Company Law* by M. C. Oliver (Revised by E. A. Marshall) M & E Handbooks (1987)

7. *Company Law for Accountants* by C. D. Thomas – 2nd Edition – Butterworths (1988)

8. *Caribbean Law and Business* Volume 2 No 1 (April 1990) pp 42 – 87

9. *Regulatory Framework of Accounting in the Caribbean* by Margaret Mendes – *CFM* Publications (1987)

10. *Company Law in the Commonwealth Caribbean: The Need For Reform* by Brynmor Pollard

11. *Report of the Review Committee on the Companies Law of Guyana* (1988)

Regional Legislation

- **ANTIGUA**

The Companies Act, Chapter 358 – Revised Laws, with amendments.

- **BAHAMAS**

The Companies Act 1992, 18/1992.

- **BARBADOS**

The Companies Act 1982 54/82 came into effect on 1/1/85.

- **BELIZE**

The Companies Ordinance, Chapter 206. Revised Laws with amendments.

- **DOMINICA**

The Companies Ordinance. Revised Laws with amendments.

- **GRENADA**

The Companies Ordinance, Chapter 47. Revised Laws.

- **GUYANA**

1. The Companies Act, Chapter 89:01. Revised Laws (still in force).
2. Companies Act 1991, 29/91 (not yet in force).

- **JAMAICA**

The Companies Act, Revised Laws with amendments.

- **MONSTERRAT**

The Companies Act, Chapter 308. Revised Laws with amendments.

- **ST. KITTS-NEVIS-ANGUILLA**

The Companies Act, Chapter 335. Revised Laws with amendments.

- **ST. LUCIA**

The Commercial Code, Chapter 244. Revised Laws with amendments.

- **ST. VINCENT**

The Companies Ordinance, Chapter 219. Revised Laws with amendments.

- **TRINIDAD AND TOBAGO**

The Companies Ordinance, Chapter 31 – No. (1). Revised Laws.

- **UNITED KINGDOM ACTS**

  Regional Statutes are originally based on the following

1862 or earlier — Antigua, the Bahamas[1], Dominica, Montserrat, St Kitts-Nevis-Anguilla, St Vincent.

1908 — Barbados[1], Belize, Grenada, Guyana[1] and St Lucia (with 1948 amendments)

1929 — Trinidad and Tobago

1948 — Jamaica

---

1. The Bahamas, Barbados and Guyana have new Companies Acts.

CHAPTER I

Introduction

The word "company" imports that an association of a number of persons is formed for some common purpose which is more or less of a permanent character. Such an association may be "incorporated"[1] or "unincorporated".

A company when incorporated, becomes a legal person, though artificial, which is separate and distinct from the members of the company. An unincorporated company is not, however, a legal entity separate from its members.

There are two principal methods of incorporating companies in the Commonwealth Caribbean Region[2] – by special Acts of Parliament[3] and by registration with the Registrar of Companies under the various Companies Acts in the region.

Each method of incorporation creates legal entities having the attributes of corporations but there are certain fundamental differences.

In order to understand the methods of incorporation, it is necessary to have some knowledge of the history of company law in England, since it is from England that, as colonies, our company law in the region was derived.

The law of an individual territory in the region varies from that of the United Kingdom and the other territories according to:

(a)   the period when the original legislation of the individual territory was enacted;

(b)   any subsequent amendments made to the legislation; *and*

(c)   whether comprehensive revision has recently been enacted.

Historical Background

The concept of incorporation has been recognized in the United Kingdom since medieval times. Earliest use was in connection with ecclesiastical and public bodies which had corporate status given to them by charters of the Crown. The trading association was a later development.

Charters had the following attributes:

(a) perpetual life;
(b) limited liability;
(c) right to sue and be sued in its corporate name;
(d) the right to enter into contracts and to acquire property in its own name.

In the commercial sphere the principal medieval associations were the Guild Merchants organizations (the medieval guilds) which correspond, roughly to trade protection associations and which were, mainly monopolies.

They were not really trading associations at all, but bodies which sought to regulate the carrying on of particular trades by their members and to preserve for their members, the monopoly of carrying on a trade in a particular locality.

The first trading associations were in the form of partnerships which were in existence before the 13th century. *Partnerships* evolved from the family business.

Trading associations known as "companies" did not appear in any numbers until the 16th century. This was due to the expansion of foreign trade, when the Crown granted *charters of incorporation* to many companies of merchant adventurers trading in various parts of the world. (Each trader traded with his own stock and on his own account.)

During the 17th century, most of these "companies" began trading as single entities on behalf of their members, each member contributing a fraction of the merchandise to be sold and taking a proportionate share of the proceeds. This form of trading was known as "Joint Stock" trading, the joint stock being the merchandise provided by the members. Such associations did not enjoy limited liability[4].

At this time the only method of obtaining incorporation was by royal charter or by an Act of Parliament, which was not easily or cheaply procured.

Consequently, many associations were *formed by agreement* without incorporation, simply by their members executing a document known as Articles of Partnership or Deed of Settlement which contained provisions similar to those found in the charters of incorporated bodies.

Up to the 17th century therefore, there was no differentiation in substance between partnerships and incorporated bodies.

At the beginning of the 18th century, there was a boom in unincorporated company floatations. This led to the South Sea Bubble scandal and the passing of the Bubble Act in 1720. The Bubble Act was the first attempt to regulate unincorporated bodies. It prohibited unincorporated trading companies from acting as trading corporations. It checked widespread speculation in shares, froze the raising of capital and the development of the capital market. However, it did not destroy the unincorporated body altogether. Unincorporated associations in the form of partnerships, grew considerably. The Bubble Act was repealed in 1825.

In 1844, the first general Companies Act was enacted by the Joint Stock Companies Act, 1844. The system of registration for Companies had its origin in this Act. The Act recognized the need for the incorporation of trading associations and for the registration of such bodies without the necessity of obtaining a royal charter or a special Act of Parliament. The Act made it compulsory to register as companies, all partnerships with more than *twenty-five members.*

Limited liability[5] was not granted until 1855 by the Limited Liability Act of 1855, which was later replaced by the Joint Stock Companies Act of 1856. The latter Act substituted two documents, the Memorandum of Association and the Articles of Association, for the Deed of Settlement or Articles of Partnership.

The 1844 Act was enacted to invest companies with some of the attributes of the corporation. It introduced three main principles which have constituted the basis of Company Law ever since:

(1) It provided for registration of companies with more than 25 members (reduced in 1856 to 20 members);

(2) It conferred legal personality (by incorporation) but not with limited liability;

(3) It provided for publicity of the company's affairs in order to protect the investing public by the establishment of the Office

of Registrar and the filing of certain documents dealing with the affairs of the company.

From then on, companies were placed on a sound legal footing though with *unlimited liability.*

The Companies Act of 1856 was repealed by the Companies Act of 1862 which was a consolidation Act with amendments. This later Act followed the same pattern but with a number of improvements. The 1862 Act became the basic method of incorporation, that is, by the registration of companies and this has remained substantially the same to this day[6].

By 1862, the major developments in Company Law were:

(i)   it was compulsory to incorporate companies with more than twenty members;

(ii) a company with seven or more members may be incorporated with limited liability;

(iii) a company registered under the law had to have a Memorandum of Association and Articles of Association.

The 1862 Act was amended several times and in 1908[7] the law was further consolidated. Further consolidations were done in 1929[8], 1948[9] and 1985.

Company Law has grown substantially in volume, coverage and complexity over the years. Successive consolidations and amendments have sought to increase the protection of investors and persons who deal with companies. Detailed registers and records were required to be kept. The Companies Act 1985 (UK) consolidates the legislation enacted between 1948 and 1983.

Companies formed under the Companies Acts have two principal features:

(1)   First, they are corporations, i.e. artificial legal persons. This means that companies may own property, enter into contracts, inflict or suffer wrongs, sue and be sued and do or have done to them, most other things which may be done by, or to a natural person.

(2)   Secondly, they enjoy limited liability in certain cases. By this it is meant that the liability of their members to contribute towards the debts of the companies is usually limited.

Case Law and the Development of Company Law

The Companies Acts were far from being a complete code. Judicial decisions played an important part in the development of certain principles of Company Law. The Companies Acts laid down general principles and procedures to be followed. The Courts however, had to interpret the law and applied these to the cases that came before them. A vast body of case law has developed thereby. The role of case law should not therefore be underestimated in the development of Company Law.

Examples of cases whereby the Courts filled some substantial gaps in the legislation in the latter part of the 19th century are:

(1)   *Foss* v *Harbottle* [1843] – where a wrong is done to a company it is the company which must take action to redress the wrong and not individual members.

(2)   *Royal British Bank* v *Turquand* [1855] – outsiders are entitled to assume that internal matters have been complied with.

(3)   *Ooregum Gold Mining Co* v *Roper* [1892] – a company cannot issue shares at a discount;

(4)   *Salomon* v *Salomon & Company* [1897] – a company is a separate legal entity from its members;

(5)   *Trevor* v *Whitworth* [1887] – a company must maintain its capital;

(6)   *Ashbury Carriage Co* v *Riche* [1875] – ultra vires doctrine;

(7)   *Erlanger's New Sombrero Phosphate Co* [1878] – promoters' duties.

Historical Position in the Caribbean Region

The Company Law of individual territories within the Region have much in common, both in their fundamental structure and in detailed provisions.

The territories have, without exception, used as a *model* for their legislation, a United Kingdom Act, and have relied upon the Case Law of the United Kingdom.

In each case, however, the model used was the Act in force in the United Kingdom at the time that the individual state drafted its legislation[10]. Though amendments were subsequently made in the United Kingdom legislation, this may not have been reflected in the local legislation. However, in spite of the common base there is a lack of homogeneity in the laws of the Region.

Report on the Harmonisation of Company Law – The CARICOM Report

In 1971, at the Eighth Meeting of the Council of Ministers of the Caribbean Free Trade Association (CARIFTA), it was decided to launch a project for the harmonisation of Company Law within Member Territories. A Working Party was appointed to carry out the project. It consisted of representatives appointed by the various governments and by the Caribbean Development Bank, the University of the West Indies, the Caribbean Association of Industry and Commerce and the CARICOM Secretariat. Dr Kenneth Rattray, Solicitor General of Jamaica, was elected Chairman. The project was continued under the Caribbean Community (CARICOM) when this institution came into existence in 1973.

A draft model legislation was prepared in 1978 by Mr W. J. Menary, in consultation with the Working Party. The final report and the model legislation were approved by the Working Party in 1979. In its report, the Working Party supported the adoption of a harmonised approach to the enactment of companies legislation within the Region and that its model legislation should be the basis for legislation.

Since the *CARICOM Report*, several countries within the Region have passed Companies Acts: Barbados in 1982; Guyana in 1991 and the Bahamas in 1992. These three adopted most of the recommendations of the Report and the provisions contained in the Draft Bill. Both Trinidad and Tobago and Jamaica are presently actively involved in the preparation of new legislation in this regard.

Barbados, however, established its own Committee. A Companies Bill was the result and this became the Companies Act of 1982. This Act has since been amended.

There are areas of difference between the *CARICOM Report,* and the Barbados legislation, though the Barbados Committee benefitted from its association with the Working Party and its discussions.

The Guyana Act is not yet in effect. It is to come into operation on such date as the Minister may, by order, appoint – see s 1 of the Act. No date has yet been decided on.

Main Recommendations contained in the CARICOM Report

(a) The introduction of "proprietary companies" instead of private companies.

(b) The introduction of the "one man" membership company.

(c) There should be a single constituent document to be called "the articles of association" instead of a memorandum and articles of association. This document is to contain the essential information of the company. Additional matters are to be dealt with in the "by-laws" of the company.

(d) The company should be enabled to adopt pre-incorporation contracts made on its behalf within a reasonable time after it comes into existence.

(e) The company should have the capacity of a natural person. Limits can be imposed in the articles of incorporation, if necessary.

(f) The ultra vires and the constructive notice doctrines should be abolished.

(g) Substitution of a system of no par value for nominal or par value shares.

(h) All shares are to be issued fully paid up and all equity shares should have voting rights.

(i) Fuller rules for the maintenance of equity or capital but with provisions for permitted reductions. In relation to the reduction of capital there should be no requirement for confirmation by the court.

(j) Disclosure of substantial shareholdings and transactions in that connection.

(k) Use of derivative action by a shareholder.

(l) Fuller protection against oppression of minorities and improper variation of class rights.

(m) Controls upon insider trading.

(n) Disqualification of directorships.

(o) Qualification of directors' shareholdings.

(p) Format of balance sheets and profit and loss accounts.

(q) Control of take-over bids.

(r) Inspection and investigations into company affairs.

(s) Regional enforcement of winding-up orders.

- **Summary of the main changes made by the Barbados Companies Act 1982 (54/82) (came into effect January 1, 1985)**

(1) Incorporation of a company by a single person is permitted.

(2) Incorporation is effected by filing "articles of incorporation".

(3) Company has the capacity of a natural person.

(4) Company does not have to state its objects and powers.

(5) Common law doctrines of ultra vires and constructive notice abolished.

(6) Shares to be issued with no par value.

(7) Company permitted to purchase its own shares subject to solvency requirements which is similar to the requirements for the paying of dividends.

(8) Pre-incorporation contracts could be adopted by company when incorporated.

(9) Directors duties and liabilities expressly set out. The general duty to act honestly and in good faith in the best interest of the company has been given statutory effect.

(10) Greater rights and more effective remedies given to minority shareholders.

(11) Rights and duties of auditors set out.

(12) Accounting procedures simplified. Fuller records to be kept.

(13) Financial disclosure to the Registrar required of all public companies or larger "private" companies (those with over $250,000 gross revenues or $1,000,000 assets).

- **GUYANA Companies Act of 1991 (29 of 1991) (Not yet brought into force)**

Substantially similar provisions as in the Barbados Companies Act of 1982.

- **BAHAMAS Companies Act of 1992 (18 of 1992) (Came into effect August 1, 1992)**

Changes made are not as wide as the Barbados or the Guyana Acts. These are more in line with the Jamaica Companies Act of 1965 (based on 1948 Act of United Kingdomwith some modern features).

MAIN CHANGES IN THE LAW

(1) *Two* or more persons may incorporate a company instead of five;

(2) Incorporation is effected by a Memorandum of Association. Articles of association may be filed with the memorandum or within six months thereafter;

(3) Company has the capacity of an individual of full capacity;

(4) Company does not have to state is objects and powers;

(5) Common law doctrine of ultra vires and constructive notice abandoned;

(6) Private companies must have at least two directors. Public companies at least three. No person who is under age or is of unsound mind or is an undischarged bankrupt may be a director;

(7) An annual return must be filed with the Registrar.

Notes

1   For incorporation of a company, see p. 21, infra.
2   Including the Bahamas, Belize and Guyana.
3   See, e.g., Building Societies Act and Friendly Societies Act.
4   An example of a joint stock trading association was the East India Company (1600).
5   See p. 17, infra.
6   Regional status originally based on the 1862 Act (U.K.) and earlier statutes are Antigua, the Bahamas, Dominica, Montserrat,
    St Kitts-Nevis-Anguilla and St Vincent.
7   Barbados, Belize, Grenada, Guyana, and St Lucia are based on the 1908 Act (U.K.).
8   Trinidad and Tobago - 1929 Act (U.K.).
9   Jamaica - 1948 Act (U.K.).
10 E.g., Antigua (1844); St Vincent (1846); Guyana (1908); Trinidad and Tobago (1925).

CHAPTER 2

Legal Forms of Business

Today, a business may be conducted in one of three ways:
- (1) by a sole trader;
- (2) by a partnership;
- (3) by a registered company.

Sole Trader and Proprietor

The sole trader is the sole person responsible for running the business and he alone enjoys the profits. He may engage others to assist him but this does not alter the fact that management of the business is in his hands. He is personally liable for debts incurred for the business and enjoys no limited liability even though he may be registered under the Registration of Business Names Act[1].

Partnership

A partnership has been defined as the legal relationship which exists between persons carrying on a business in common with a view of making a profit without being incorporated.

Generally speaking, no registration is required in order to form a partnership but note should be made of the Registration of Business Names Act which requires persons trading under a name other than their surname to register under that Act.

Partners are called, collectively, a firm and the name in which the business is carried on is referred to as the firm's name.

Under the law, a partnership is not a legal entity, as is the case of a company registered under the Companies Act. The firm's name is merely a convenient expression for the collective names of the individual partners.

The names of the existing partners need not be the same as the firm's name; for persons can carry on a business under any name they please, provided they are in compliance with the law of the land.

In deciding whether or not a partnership exists, one must look at he nature of the relationship and not the label attached to it. This is a question of fact.

Partnerships are most common among the professions and certain trades which are prevented by their organizations from operating through the medium of a registered company enjoying limited liability at the expense of their clients.

Partnership is created by agreement between the partners. This may be oral or implied from the conduct of the parties or it may be written in the form of Articles of Partnership or Deed of Partnership.

The general practice is to have a written agreement setting out clearly the terms of the partnership including the rights and obligations of a partner.

The legislation in the Region commonly restricts the number of persons who can form a partnership[2]. Where this number is exceeded, a business must be registered as a company under the Companies Act or must be registered under some other statute.

Registered Company

The modern usage of the word "company" is generally to describe a company formed by registration under the various Companies Acts in the Region. The following text is concerned with this type of company and follows this usage.

Main characteristics of a registered company

The main characteristics of a registered company are:

(1) It is a legal entity separate from its members;

(2) It enjoys limited liability, if so registered;

(3) It has perpetual succession i.e. a change in the membership does not affect the existence of the company;

(4) Being an artificial entity it can only be managed by natural persons called directors;

(5) It has a written constitution;

(6) It must be registered with the Registrar of Companies;

(7) Its assets and liabilities are its own and not its members.

Main differences between a Partnership and a Registered Company

(1) A partnership is not a separate legal entity (i.e. there is no separate existence distinct from its members). A company is a legal person though artificial in nature.

(2) A partnership does not have perpetual succession but a company has. A change in membership does not affect the existence of a company, but a change in the membership in a partnership does.

(3) In the formation of a company, certain documents must be filed with the Registrar of Companies and certain fees must be paid. In a partnership this does not have to be done.

(4) A partnership has no common seal but a company has.

(5) Partnership property is generally jointly owned by the partners. The property owed by the company belongs to the company and not its members.

(6) Partners can do any business they agree on once its lawful but a company is subject to the ultra vires doctrine i.e. it cannot act beyond its powers as provided in its memorandum of association.

(7) Partners are liable jointly for the contractual liabilities and obligations of the firm. The liability of a member of a

company is normally limited to the extent of the unpaid amount on his shares with the company.

(8) Partners can take part in the management of the firm – members of a company cannot. The directors of a company are responsible for its management.

(9) Partnership affairs are private – companies are subject to the Companies Act and certain information must be filed with the Registrar of Companies.

(10) A partnership cannot create a floating charge over its assets; companies can.

(11) Tax liability and relief may differ in a partnership and a company.

(12) The property of a partnership belongs to partners in common. Property of a company is owned by the company and not by individual members.

(13) Partners are agents of each other and the firm. The members of a company are not its agents.

(14) The formation of a partnership is a simple matter. It can be formed merely by an agreement. A company must file certain documents with the Registrar of Companies and obtain a Certificate of Incorporation.

(15) A partnership can be dissolved by a partner simply giving notice. A company must be wound up in accordance with the Companies Act.

Notes

1. Registration under the Registration of Business Names Act does not confer corporate status.
2. For example, in Jamaica the number is 20.

CHAPTER 3

Characteristics of a Registered Company

Separate Legal Personality

The essence of a registered company is that it has a legal personality which is separate from its members. This separate personality[1] is referred to as "the veil of incorporation". If the membership changes, the company still retains its identity as a legal entity.

The existence of a separate legal personality is at the heart of company law. The legal basis for the separate legal personality doctrine is to be found in the case of *Salomon v Salomon and Co* [1897] AC 22.

> Mr. Salomon was a boot and shoe manufacturer in business for a number of years. He converted his business into a limited liability company. As part of the purchase price for the business, he took shares in the company for a part of the money and took debentures for the remainder. The debentures entitled him to a fixed charge on the company's assets. Immediately on the formation of the company trade went into depression. To keep afloat the company borrowed money. However, the company had to go into liquidation. Because of his fixed charge Mr Salomon claimed for his loan to the company over the other creditors. The liquidator tried to have Mr Salomon's claim set aside as being fraudulent and that Mr Salomon was basically the company. The case went to the House of Lords which held that the company was a separate legal person from Mr Salomon and that Mr Salomon as a member was not personally liable for the loans made by the creditors to the company.

In the *Salomon* case, the House of Lords in 1897 recognised that Parliament had permitted the creation of corporations as distinct legal entities separate from the individual members. As a result of this case, the courts have generally considered themselves bound by the concept that a company is a separate legal person distinct from its members and would not generally go behind the veil of incorporation.

Piercing or Lifting the Corporate Veil

Notwithstanding the company's "veil of incorporation" the courts have, in certain cases "pierced" or "lifted" the corporate veil and looked behind it to see who controls the company and have, in certain circumstances, held those persons liable instead of the company. No consistent policy has been followed and it cannot be predicted with any certainty whether or not the court will lift the veil in any particular case. The clearest justification for the court to go behind the veil is to do justice in a particular matter. The courts have intervened where there is a flagrant disregard for justice, to prevent fraud to protect the revenue and in cases where the nature of the persons who control it is a relevant factor, e.g. where they are enemies.

In *Lennard's Carrying Co. Ltd.* v *Asiatic Petroleum Co. Ltd.* [1915] AC 705 at 713 Viscount Haldane said:

> "A corporation is an abstraction. It has no mind of its own any more than it has a body of its own; its active and directing will must consequently be sought in the person of somebody who, for some purpose may be called an agent, but who is really the directing mind and will of the corporation, the very ego and centre of the personality of the corporation."

In *Littlewoods Mail Order Stores Ltd.* v *I.R.C.* [1969] 3 ALLER 855 Lord Demming said:

> "The doctrine laid down in *Salomon* v *Salomon & Co. Ltd.* has to be watched very carefully. It has often been supposed to cast a veil over the personality of a limited company through which the courts cannot see. But that is not true. The courts can and often do draw aside the veil. They can and often do, pull off the masks. They look to see what really lies behind".

The following are examples where the veil of the incorporation has been lifted:

1   *Where the corporate veil is used for fraud, illegality or*
     improper purpose.

In *Jones* v *Lipman* [1962] 1 ALLER 442 the defendant had contracted to sell his house to the plaintiff. In order to avoid having to complete the sale, he transferred it to a company which he controlled. An order for specific performance of the contract of sale was made against the defendant and the company. In this case, the court considered that the company was nothing but a "cloak", "sham" or "mask" for the defendant.

In *Torquay Hotel Co.* v *Cousins* [1969] 2 Ch 106, the directors of a company were held personally liable for intentionally rendering the fulfillment of a contract by the company impossible. The defendants sought to escape liability by pleading that they acted merely as agents, but the court considered itself free to look behind the corporate veil and act on the realities of the situation.

2   *Where the court needs to ascertain some physical or mental*
     attitude and it is necessary to look at the human management
     involved in the control of the company for this (i.e. the "alter
     ego" of the company).

In *Daimler Co. Ltd.* v *Continental Tyre and Rubber Co. Ltd.* [1916] 2 AC 307 H.L. the respondent sued Daimler for money due in respect of goods supplied. Daimler's defence was that to pay the debt was to trade with the enemy as the members and officers were Germans and at the time there was war between England and Germany. Despite the fact that the company was registered in England, the defence succeeded. The question which arose in this case was whether in times of war a company incorporated in England but controlled by enemy subjects can itself be an enemy.

Difficulty sometimes lies in determining who is the "alter ego" of the company. As the company is an artificial person created by a legal fiction human beings must act and think for it. Sometimes it is difficult to distinguish whether the actions and thoughts of these persons are the actions and thoughts of those persons as individuals or are those of the company. This poses particular problems, more so, in the case of the "one man company" as in the *Salomon's* case where the main shareholder, the single director and the employee can be one and the same person and that person is also the main creditor. (See *Lee* v *Lee's Air Farming Ltd.* [1961] AC 12)

3   *Consideration of the relationship between a holding company and its* subsidiary.

In *Smith, Stone & Knight Ltd.* v *Birmingham Corp.* [1939] 4 ALLER 116 the plaintiff company acquired a partnership business and formed it into a company of which the plaintiff was the controlling shareholder. The profits of the new company were treated as the plaintiff's profits. In proceedings brought against the defendant, the court held that the plaintiff as the holding company was the proper party.

4   *In revenue matters a company's residence is one of the main factors in determining its liability to pay tax. The location of the company's central control and management is crucial to the determination of the company's residence.*

In *Unit Construction Co. Ltd.* v *Bullock* [1960] it was held that the subsidiaries of the company though incorporated outside of the United Kingdom (U.K.) were controlled and managed by their parent company in the U.K. and therefore were resident in the U.K.

Property

A company can own property both real and personal. A company's property is separate from that of its members. A member has no proprietary right to the property of the company and a creditor of the company can only claim against the property of the company.

In *Macaura* v *Nothern Assurance Co. Ltd.* (1925) it was held that since the company's property belonged to the company, no individual member has any insurable interest in the property.

Limited Liability

Though generally a company is a separate legal person and therefore is liable, without limit, for its debts, the majority of companies are registered on the basis of limited liability by shares, i.e. the liability of shareholders is limited on a winding up of the company, to the extent of any amount owing on their shares with the company.

Perpetual Succession

A company has perpetual succession, i.e. it will continue in existence until it is dissolved as provided under the Companies Act, e.g. by the process of winding up. Its existence is independent of its members. A change in the membership has no effect on its existence.

Criminal and Civil Liability

A registered company being a legal person under the law may incur liabilities like any other person.

Criminal Liability

The criminal liability of a registered company is somewhat uncertain. This is because of the general rule that a person cannot be liable for a criminal act without the mental condition known as "mens rea", i.e. guilty knowledge.

A company being an artificial entity can have no mind of its own to have knowledge. However, it has been held that when a crime has been committed by a senior officer of the company (not necessarily a director), who can be treated as the "directing mind and will" of the company then the company can itself be found to be guilty of the crime.

Many statutes also impose criminal liability on a company for offences committed by its agents (i.e. its officers and employees). There are some offences which it is inconceivable that a company can commit, e.g. rape and bigamy.

A company being an artificial person can only be punished by a fine and not by imprisonment.

In *H. L. Bolton (Engineering) Co. Ltd.* v *T. J. Graham & Sons Ltd.* [1957] QB 159 Lord Justice Denning said:

> "A company may in many ways be likened to a human body. It has a brain and
> a nerve centre which controls what it does. It also has hands which hold tools
> and act in accordance with directions from the centre. Some of the people in
> the company are mere servants and agents who are nothing more than hands to
> do the work and cannot be said to represent the mind or will. Others are
> directors and managers who represent the directing mind and will of the

company, and control what it does. The state of mind of these managers is the state of mind of the company and is treated by the law as such".

In *Tesco Supermarkets* v *Nattrass* [1972] AC 153 Tesco had been convicted of an offence under the Trade Descriptions Act for selling a product at a price higher than the advertised price. Tesco was entitled to a defence if it could be shown (amongst other things) that the offence was committed by "another person". Tesco alleged that the "other person" in this case was the manager of the branch involved who had been in sole command of that store. The court held that the manager was not "another person" for the purposes of the defence and that the company could properly be convicted for the offence.

In *DPP* v *Kent and Sussex Contractors Ltd.* [1944] KB 146, the Divisional Court held that a company could properly be convicted of an offence which required proof of an intent to deceive. The intention was that of the transport manager of the company whose knowledge must be imported to the company as he was its agent.

Each case will turn on its own facts and depend upon the precise nature of the distribution of power within the particular company. For example, the case of *Moore* v *Bresler Ltd.* [1944] 2 ALLER 559 has been criticised on the grounds that the court went 'too far down the scale' in convicting a company of tax fraud where that fraud was carried out by the company secretary and the manager of one branch. In view of the enhanced status of the company secretary today (see chapter 7) that criticism may be of less force today.

Civil Liability

A test similar to that used in criminal liability is used to determine the civil liability of a company both in contract and in tort. It must be remembered, however, that the principle of vicarious liability in civil law is much more widely used and so there may be that route to liability as well as the use of the "alter ego" doctrine.

In *Lennard's Carrying Company Ltd.* v *Asiatic Petroleum Co. Ltd.* [1915] AC 705, the *alter ego* doctrine was the basis of the company's liability. The question was whether damage had occurred without "the actual fault or privity" of the owner of the ship. The owners were a company. The fault was that of the registered managing owner who managed the ship on behalf of the owners. It was held that Mr Lennard was the directing mind of the company so that his fault was the fault of the company. (See also *Campbell* v *Paddington Corporation* [1911] 1 KB 869 and *The Lady Gwendolyn* [1965] P 294.)

Note

1. As a result of the existence of this separate legal personality, the company's property is owned by the company and not the members, and its business is conducted by the company and not the members.

CHAPTER 4

Incorporation

The Formation of a Company

Regional companies' statutes provide generally for the creation of three types of companies that can be registered:

(1)   companies limited by shares;
(2)   companies limited by guarantee;
(3)   unlimited companies.

Companies Limited by Shares

A Company limited by shares is one in which the liability of a shareholder is limited to the amount unpaid, if any, on his shares with the company. The vast majority of registered companies fall within this class. This characteristic as well as the capacity to have a share capital are attractive features for business enterprises.

Companies Limited by Guarantee

A company limited by guarantee is one in which the members agree to contribute towards the winding-up of the company a certain amount of money which is stated in the memorandum of association. Such a company is usually non-profit making in character and is concerned with charitable matters, i.e. educational, religious or other similar matters. Such companies have little advantage over a company limited by shares and are rare.

Unlimited Companies

In an unlimited company, the shareholders are fully liable for the debts of the company. It is similar in form to partnerships. Such companies are comparatively rare today.

The vast majority of companies are companies limited by shares and this book is concerned mainly with these companies. It should be borne in mind, however, that the Companies Acts of the Region are of general application.

Private and Public Companies

The more modern Companies Acts of the Region allow for each type of company to be formed either as a private company or a public company[1].

In the older legislation, private companies were not recognized as such. See, for example, the legislation of St. Vincent, where the statute is silent, although in practice a private company could be created by drafting an appropriate memorandum and articles of association.

To form a private company, the following conditions usually have to be fulfilled:

(a) the right to transfer the shares of the company should be restricted;

(b) the maximum number of members should be restricted (in some territories, this is fifty; in others it is twenty)[2];

(c) any invitation to the public to subscribe for shares or debentures in the company is prohibited.

These restrictions are to be found in the companies' articles.

Companies which cannot meet these conditions are public companies. The vast majority of companies in the Region are private companies, mostly family concerns.

Privileges of Private Companies

Generally, a private company:

(a) may be registered and carry on business with a minimum of *two* members. In case of public companies, the minimum number is seven[3]. (In the older legislation, the minimum number for all companies is seven. The "one man" company is now to be found in the Barbados, Bahamas and Guyana legislations.)[4]

(b) need not file a prospectus or a statement in lieu of prospectus[5] before it commences business on incorporation;

(c) need have only one director and a secretary as against *two* directors and a secretary for public companies. (In the Bahamas private companies must have at least two directors and public companies at least three.)

(d) can commence business as soon as it is incorporated;

(e) does not have to hold a statutory meeting or to issue and file a *statutory report* soon after commencement of business or incorporation as is required for a private company.

(f) is exempt from filing a copy of its accounts with the Registrar of Companies.

Conversion of a Private Company to a Public Company

Generally, a company will cease to be a private company if it alters its articles by removing the restrictions imposed under the Act in order to be a private company, and within the prescribed time after the date of alteration, deliver to the Registrar of Companies for registration, a prospectus[6] (or a statement in lieu of prospectus, if provided) in the prescribed form.

Further, if a private company is in default of any of the restrictions required to be a private company the company ceases to be a private company.

The company must pass a special resolution[7] that it should be re-registered as a public company. The special resolution must make the necessary changes to the articles.

An application to re-register must be sent to the Registrar. This must be signed by a director or secretary and must be accompanied by the amended articles and the special resolution.

A change of status from a private to a public company is more common than registration as a public company at the initial registration stage.

The practice is to initially register as a private company and subsequently convert to a public company when the capital requirements are beyond the resources of its members and their circle.

The fundamental difference between public and private companies is that only public companies may invite the public to subscribe for shares in the company.

A public company is more suitable for inviting investment by large numbers of persons. A private company is suitable for running a business in which a small number of persons are involved.

The regulations governing public companies are more extensive than those governing private companies. In a number of areas, however, no distinction is made.

Documents for Incorporation

Whether a company is a public company or a private company, for it to be incorporated, certain documents must be filed with the Registrar of Companies.

The Memorandum of Association and Articles of Association

In the early history of companies, the constitution and the internal rules of management were contained in one document – the Deed of Settlement or Articles of Partnership. In modern times, except for Barbados[8] and Guyana[9], the usual requirement in order to effect registration is to file with the Registrar of Companies *two* main documents. These are the Memorandum of Association[10] and the Articles of Association[11].

The memorandum contains the constitution and powers (i.e. fundamental law) of the Company and the articles[12] deal with the internal rules of management of the company.

Barbados and Guyana in their recent legislations have adopted the recommendation contained in the CARICOM Report. Only one principal constituent document – "the Articles of Incorporation" – is required to be filed with the Registrar of Companies.

In addition to the memorandum and articles, a public company with a share capital is required to lodge the following with the Registrar of Companies:

    (a)   a consent to act as director signed by a person who is appointed as a director;

    (b)   a list of the directors who have consented to act as such;

    (c)   an undertaking by the directors to take up the required qualification shares, if this is required.

Statutory Declaration of Compliance

In addition to the filing of the memorandum of association and the articles of association, a statutory declaration of compliance with all the requirements is also to be filed with the Registrar by the attorney-at-law who is engaged in the formation of the company or by a person named as a director or a secretary of the company.

If an attorney-at-law is not employed in the formation of the company, it will be essential that at least one director or the secretary is named in the articles of association; otherwise there will be no qualified person to make the declaration of compliance.

The Registrar may accept the declaration as sufficient evidence of compliance with the provisions of the Act.

Registration formalities of a Company

(1)   Generally seven in the case of a public company or *two* in the case of a private company or more persons associated for any lawful purpose may, by subscribing their names to a memorandum of association and otherwise complying with the requirements of the Companies Act in respect of registration form a company with or without limited liability. (The "one man" company is now to be found in Barbados and Guyana).

(2)   The signatures of the subscribers to the memorandum must be witnessed by at least one person;

(3)   The memorandum must be duly stamped with stamp duty;

(4)   The residential addresses and the description of the subscribers must be given;

(5) The subscribers must subscribe for at least one share each, even if they intend to take a large number of shares;

(6) The subscribers need not sign at the same time or in the presence of each other;

(7) Each subscriber must write opposite his name, the number of shares he has taken;

(8) The same witness need not attest to all the signatures. He must give his name and address. He need not state his description.

Procedure for Registration

The promoters of a company or their advisers will draw up the company's constitutional documents – namely the memorandum of association and the articles of association or articles of incorporation as the case may be. These and other documents are submitted to the Registrar of Companies who will register the documents on payment of certain fees and stamp duties. The Registrar must satisfy himself that the documents have complied with the statutory requirements. If satisfied, the Registrar will issue a certificate of incorporation.

Refusal of Registration

The area of discretion left to the Registrar of Companies for refusing an application for registration of a company is very limited. If the following apply:

(a) the minimum number of subscribers;

(b) the memorandum and the articles of association are in compliance with the legislation;

(c) the name is not undesirable; and

(d) the purpose is not unlawful;

then, the Registrar must register the company[13].

Certificate of Incorporation

On the registration of the required documents of the company with the Registrar of Companies, the Registrar will issue a Certificate of Incorporation if satisfied that the requirements were complied with.

The Certificate will state that the company is incorporated and, in the case of a limited company, that the company is limited.

On the issuance of a certificate of incorporation, the company becomes an incorporated body, known by the name in the memorandum, having an independent, legal existence with perpetual succession and a common seal. It can own property, enter into contracts and can sue and be sued in its own name, independent of its membership.

The company's existence as a legal person is unchallengeable from the date of issue of the certificate of incorporation.

The Certificate of Incorporation is the "birth certificate" of the company. It will need to be produced at various times during the lifetime of the company. The certificate is conclusive proof of the incorporation of the company from the date shown on it. On receiving its Certificate of Incorporation a private company may commence business. A public company must, however, obtain a further certificate from the Registrar that it is entitled to do so. This is only issued after the Registrar is satisfied that the provisions relating to public companies are complied with.

Barbados

- **Incorporation (See sections 4-8 of the Barbados Companies Act of 1982)**

For the incorporation of a company in Barbados, one or more persons may do this by signing and sending the *Articles of Incorporation* to the Registrar. The Company Regulations of 1982 contain model **by-laws** which can be adopted by a company.

The articles of incorporation do not have to set out the objects of the company since by section 17 of the Barbados Act the company is given the capacity of a natural person.

The articles of incorporation must follow the prescribed form[14] and must set out:

(a) the proposed name of the company;

(b) the classes and the maximum number of shares that the company is authorized to issue;

(c) if the right to transfer share is restricted, a statement to this effect and the nature of the restrictions;

(d) the number of directors;

(e) any restrictions on the business that the company may carry on.

The articles of incorporation are to be accompanied with a *statutory declaration* by an attorney-at-law stating that to the best of his knowledge and belief, no signatory to the articles is an individual who is prohibited under the Act to form or join in the formation of a company.

Guyana

- **Incorporation**
  (See sections 4 – 8 of the Guyana Companies Act of 1991)
  (not yet in force).

Similar provisions as in the case of Barbados, except that the articles of incorporation must set out also the following particulars:

(a) that the registered office of the company is to be situated in Guyana

and

(b) the minimum issue price in respect of shares or classes of shares.

Specimen Declaration of Compliance (used in Jamaica)

THE COMPANIES ACT

Declaration of compliance with the requirements of the Companies Act, on application for registration of company

Pursuant to Section

COMPANY LIMITED

I,   whose true place of abode and postal address
is   in the
                                        do solemnly and sincerely
declare that I am a person named in the Articles of Association as a Director
of the   Company Limited and that all the
requirements of the Companies Act,   in respect of matters
precedent to the registration of the said company and incidental thereto
have been complied with.

AND I make this solemn declaration conscientiously believing the same to be
true and by virtue of the Voluntary Declarations Act.

Declared at   )
)
in the Parish of   )
)
this   day of   )
)
Before me:)
)
)
)
)

JUSTICE OF THE PEACE OF FOR THE PARISH OF

Specimen Certificate of Incorporation (Jamaica)

CERTIFICATE OF INCORPORATION OF A COMPANY

I hereby CERTIFY that

was INCORPORATED under the

Companies Act as a LIMITED Company

on the day of

One thousand

Given under my hand at Kingston this   day of

One thousand nine hundred and

REGISTRAR OF COMPANIES

No of Company

Notes

1. The Companies Act of 1907 created the category of "private" company with a minimum membership of two.
2. Originally, it was 25 members at least — later reduced to at least 20 members.
3. For Bahamas it was five but it is now two.
4. See p. 7, supra.
5. See p. 92, infra.
6. See p. 92, infra.
7. See p. 134, infra.
8. Barbados may incorporate a company by sending "Articles of Incorporation" to the Registrar - see p. 27, infra.
9. Guyana has similar provisions as in the case of Barbados Act - see s 4 of 1991 Act (but this is not yet in force).
10. See p. 32, infra.
11. See p. 49, infra.
12. See Table A, p. 54, infra.
13. In R. v Registrar of Companies ex parte Attorney General [1991] the application for registration was for the unlawful purpose of prostitution and was refused by the Registrar. See also R.v. Registrar of Companies, ex parte, Bowen (1914) 3 KB 116; and ex parte Moore (1931) 2 KB 197.
14. See Form I in the Third Schedule of the Companies Regulations 1984 (Barbados).

CHAPTER 5

The Memorandum of Association

The categories of information required in the Region for the memorandum of association[1] of a limited liability company are basically the same. The memorandum of association must state:

(a) the proposed name of the company;
(b) that the registered office of the company is to be situated in the territory;
(c) the objects of the company;
(d) that liability of the members is limited;
(e) the nominal share capital of the company and its division into shares of a fixed amount;
(f) the subscribers (subscription clause).

There must also be shown in the memorandum, against the name of each subscriber, the number of shares he takes, being at least one share. The memorandum must be signed by each subscriber and his signature must be witnessed.

[Specified forms are to be found in the Schedules of the Acts (Table B.)]

The Name of the Company

A company being an artificial person, can only be identified by a registered name.

The company's name is to be stated in the memorandum.

Under the Registration of Business Names Act of a territory, if a business is carried on in the territory under a business name which is not its true name, the business name must be registered under that Act if not otherwise registered.

In some legislations, the Registrar is given the power to refuse to register a new company or to request it to change its name, where the name too closely resembles the name of an existing company or where it is calculated to deceive or is a kind prohibited by the legislation. In addition, as in Jamaica, the Registrar may have the power to refuse to register a company by a name which the Registrar considers "undesirable". In such a case, a right of appeal is given. (See *Crown Continental Bank Jamaica Ltd.* v *Registrar of Companies* [1972] 19 W.I.R. 473.)

Before registering a company, it may therefore be necessary to check with the Registrar that there is no objection to the name. The court can grant an injunction, as in *Ewing* v *Buttercup Margarine Co. Ltd.* [1917], where the two separate businesses are unconnected.

In the case of companies where the members' liability is limited, companies are required to end their names with the word "Limited" or with the abbreviation "Ltd.". In Barbados "corporation" or "incorporated" or the abbreviated form "corp." or "inc." may now be used in the alternative. This requirement can be waived by the Government in the case of charitable and non-profit making companies.

Passing Off

One restriction on the selection of a name for a company is imposed by the common law doctrine of "passing off", i.e. using a name so similar to the name used by an existing business as to be likely to mislead the public into confusing the two concerns. In *Exxon Corporation* v *Exxon Insurance Consultants International Ltd.* [1982] Ch 119, the Court granted an injunction restraining the defendants from using the word "Exxon" in the Company's name.

Change of Name

A company may change its name by special resolution[2] and with the approval of the Registrar. A certified copy of the special resolution is to be sent to the Registrar. An altered Certificate of Incorporation on change of name will be issued to take effect from the date of the altered certificate. A change of name takes effect from the date on which the altered certificate was issued. Notice of change of name is to be published in the Gazette and a daily newspaper circulated in the territory. A change of name does not affect the legal position of the company.

Publication of Names

It is compulsory for a company to have its name:
- (a) outside places where business is carried on;
- (b) on all letters, orders, invoices, notices, receipts;
- (c) on its seal;
- (d) on negotiable instruments.

Registered Office

In some territories in the Region the memorandum of association must state the place where the registered office is to be situated. Others merely require that the memorandum must state that the registered office is to be situated within the territory.

In most cases, a period is allowed for setting up the registered office, e.g. the day business commenced or twenty-eight days after incorporation, whichever is earlier.

A company's registered office is an important link in the administrative machinery. It is the place where all communication must be sent and certain registers and documents are to be kept. It fixes the nationality and domicile of the company.

"Domicile" of a company is the place where the company was registered; this domicile remains with the company throughout its existence. A company can only have one domicile.

"Residence" of a company is where the company carries on its business, i.e. the place of its central management and control[3]. This will usually be the place where the board of directors of the company meet.

A company may have more than one residence. The importance of a residence is with regard to taxation matters.

The importance of the registered office is that it is the address where writs may be served on the company and where documents and other communications may be sent.

The head office of a company need not be where the company is registered. It is usually the place where substantial business is carried on by the company.

A change of address of the registered office may only be made within the territory. The Registrar of Companies must be notified of any change[4] and an entry made in the register. The registered address must be stated on all business letters and forms.

Documents and registers
to be kept at registered office

The following documents and registers are usually required to be kept at the registered office:

1   Register of members
2   Register of directors and secretary
3   Register of directors' interests in shares and debentures
4   Register of debenture holders
5   Register of charges
6   Copies of instruments creating charges
7   Minute book of general meetings
8   Minute book of directors' meetings
9   Accounting records

The Objects Clause of the Company

Every company[5] is required to state its objects in the memorandum of association and a company's certificate of incorporation is conclusive evidence that the memorandum states the objects of the company.

Unlike a natural person who can do almost anything so long as it is not unlawful, a company's capacity to do things is limited to its objects clause.

The objects clause is therefore of great importance. It defines and delimits the permissible activities of the company and determines the capacity of the company. It is of importance to know whether any particular transaction is *intra* (within) or *ultra* (outside) *vires* the objects clause of the company, for on this depends its validity, as a company can only pursue its objects.

The intention of the objects clause is to serve two purposes:

(1)   as a protective device whereby shareholders and creditors are told the type of business the company is involved in

(2)   to show that the funds of the company cannot be used for purposes outside the objects clause because of the doctrine of ultra vires evolved by the courts.

The courts will construe the objects clause reasonably and in recent years objects clauses have been construed in an increasingly liberal manner. Today the courts are likely to take a wider view of what is within the company's objects.

Doctrine of Ultra Vires

Under the *doctrine of ultra vires*, a company incorporated within the Region has the legal capacity to do only such acts or carry out such transactions as are expressly or by reasonable implication authorized by the company's objects clause in the memorandum of association[6].

Any act of the company outside the ambit of the objects clause is ultra vires and void and no such act can be ratified even by the unanimous consent of all the members – *Ashbury Railway Carriage and Iron Co.* v *Riche* [1875] LR 7 HL 653. However, such powers will be implied as are incidental or conducive to the expressed objects of the company (*Rolled Steel Products [Holdings] Ltd.* v *British Steel Corporation* [1986] Ch 246).

In *Ashbury Railway Carriage & Iron Co.* v *Riche* [1875] LR 7 HL 653 the memorandum gave the company the power to make and sell railway carriages. The company entered into a contract to construct a railway in Belgium. Later the company repudiated the contract and was sued for breach of contract. The company's defence was that the contract was ultra vires and void as it was outside the objects clause of the memorandum. The court held that the contract made by the company was outside the objects of the company and was not binding on the company. Indeed the court went further and decided that such a contract could not be rendered binding on the company even though it was expressly consented to by all the shareholders, i.e. ratified by members.

(A distinction should be made between the lack of corporate capacity and the lack of capacity on the part of the directors or other officers of the company. In the latter case, the company could ratify the acts of the directors as agents of the company or the Rule in Turquand's Case may be applicable (see p. 78 *ante*). In addition, agency rules as to usual or ostensible authority may be applicable to the acts of the directors – see *Freeman & Lockyer* v *Buckhurst Park Properties (Mangal) Ltd.* [1964] & QB 480.)

The "Main Objects" Rule

In order to avoid the operation of the doctrine of ultra vires, it is not unusual today to set out several objects in the objects clause. If this is the case, the first object is regarded by the courts as the main object or substratum of the company and what follows is construed as ancillary to the main object. This interpretation is referred to as "the main objects rule".

To avoid the main objects rule, it became the practice to list a wide variety of objects and conclude with a sub-clause called an "independent objects clause" to the effect that all the objects are to be regarded as main objects and that the failure of any one of them will not prevent the company from carrying on with the others.

This was done in *Cotman* v *Brougham* [1918] AC 514 where there were 30 objects clauses in the company's memorandum enabling the company to carry on almost any kind of business. The final objects clause concluded with a declaration that every clause should be construed as a substantive clause and not limited or restricted by reference to any other clause, and that none of the clauses should be held to be subsidiary or auxiliary to the objects stated in the first clause. This last clause was there to avoid a construction restricting a widely drawn objects clause to the "main objects" rule. The House of Lords held that the transaction which was questioned was valid as being *intra vires* the objects clause and that each clause must be construed independently.

In *Re Horsley and Weight Ltd.* [1982] Ch 442, Buckley L.J. said:

> "It has long been a common practice to set out in the Memorandum of Association a great number and variety of 'objects' so called . . ."

In *Bell Houses Ltd.* v *City Wall Properties Ltd.* [1966] 2 Q B 656 the company's memorandum contained a sub-clause in its objects clause allowing it to "carry on any other trade or business whatsoever which can, in the opinion of the board of directors, be advantageously carried on by the company in connection with or as ancillary to any of the other businesses or general business of the company". With reference to this sub-clause, the Court of Appeal in England held that the directors, if they acted bona fide, could act as provided therein.

In that case, the main business of the plaintiff company was that of developing housing estates. There was no "independent objects" clause in its memorandum as in *Cotman* v *Brougham*. In an isolated transaction the company contracted with another company to introduce a financier to that company for a fee. After the introduction no fee was paid. It was held that since the directors were honestly of the opinion that the transaction could be advantageously carried out by the company, it was *intra vires* even though there was no "independent objects" clause.

In commenting on the case, Danckwerts L.J. said:

> "On the balance of authorities, it would appear that the opinion of the directors if, bona fide, can dispose of the matter and why should it not decide the matter? The shareholders subscribe their money on the basis of the Memorandum of Association and if that confers the power on the directors to decide whether in their opinion it is proper to undertake particular business in the circumstances specified, why should not their decision be binding?"

For an extensive review of the authorities, see *Rolled Steel Products* v *British Steel Corporation* [1985] Ch 246, Slade LJ's judgement.

The Power to Borrow

In *Introductions Ltd.* v *National Provincial Bank Ltd.* [1970] Ch 199, the main object of the company was to provide entertainment services for tourists and there was a provision in the objects clause which said that the company could "borrow or raise money in such manner as the company shall think fit". There was also a sub-clause which declared that each sub-clause in the objects clause is to be construed independently. In spite of this, the court held that this power to borrow should be restricted to "the purposes of the company" and in the particular case the borrowing was *ultra vires*. Consequently, the contract involved in the borrowing was void.

The justification for this is that borrowing money cannot be an object by itself. It must be done in order to further another purpose of the company.

Gratuitous Payments

In *Parke* v *Daily News Ltd.* [1961] gratuitous payments to the employees of a company who had become redundant on an amalgamation was held ultra vires. The court decided that ex gratia payments out of the assets of a company are only *intra vires* if they are:
1. bona fide;
2. reasonably incidental to the carrying on of the company's business; and
3. made for the benefit and prosperity of the company.

However, in *Re Horsley* and *Weight Ltd.* [1982], it was said that if an act is expressly authorized by the memorandum, the question of whether it will benefit or promote the prosperity of the company is irrelevant. It is a question of the construction of the Memorandum. In this case the company's objects expressly included a power to grant pensions to its employees and to its directors. It was held that the power to grant pensions was a substantive object and was valid. There is no reason why a company should not part with its funds gratuitously or for non-commercial reasons if such is within its declared objects. Of this Buckley L. J. said:

> "The objects of a company do not need to be commercial; they can be charitable or philanthropic; indeed they can be whatever the original incorporators wished, provided they are legal."

In *Rolled Steel Products* v *British Steel Corporation* [1985], Slade L.J. said:

> "The basic rule is that a company incorporated under the Companies Acts only has the capacity to do those acts which fall within its objects as set out in its Memorandum of Association or are reasonably incidental to the attainment or pursuit of those objects. Ultimately, therefore, the question whether a particular transaction is within or outside its capacity must depend on the true construction of the Memorandum".

In *Simmonds* v *Heffer* [1983] BCLC 298 it was emphasized that donating money for exhibitions and sporting events cannot be within the objects of a railway company without it being expressly stated.

Potential benefit to the company or the fact that something is done in good faith is not enough. The test is what is reasonably incidental to and within the reasonable scope of the business of the company.

In *Re Lee Behrens & Co Ltd* [1932] 2 Ch 46, it was stated that three questions are to be answered:

1. Is the transaction reasonably incidental to the carrying on of the company's business?
2. Is it a bona fide transaction?
3. Is it done for the benefit and to promote the prosperity of the company?

In considering the objects of a company, the court will not simply imply a power to do something which is not for the benefit of the company – *Parke* v *Daily News* [1962].

Note, however, that if an act is within the expressed objects of a company, then it cannot be said to be outside the objects – *Re Horsley and Weight Ltd.* [1982] Ch 442.

Modern statutes have expressed provisions allowing for gratuitous payments to be made to employees of the company.

Doctrine of Constructive Notice

Under the doctrine of constructive notice, anyone dealing with the company is deemed to have constructive notice of the contents of any document required to be filed with the Registrar of Companies, even though he has not seen the document. Further, such a person is taken to have understood it according to its proper meaning. It is to be remembered that the memorandum of association is a document to be filed with the Registrar.

Everyone dealing with the company is therefore presumed to know the company's powers and the procedures and requirements to carry out these powers and the objects of the company as stated in the memorandum filed with the Registrar.

Comment

The objects clause of a company was intended to protect the shareholders by limiting the purposes for which their investments could be used and by giving protection to persons dealing with the company, such as creditors, so as to enable them to know the extent of the company's powers.

In order to avoid transactions of a company being rendered *ultra vires* and void it has become the practice to draft the objects clause as widely as possible to cover any conceivable form of activity which the company may wish to pursue in the future.

The result has been that the protection intended for shareholders and creditors has become illusory. In practice, the two doctrines of ultra vires and constructive notice operate in favour of, rather than as a protection against, the company.

Recommendations contained in the CARICOM Report

Doctrine of Ultra Vires

The *CARICOM Report* recommended the abolition of the *ultra vires* doctrine as the doctrine had outlived its usefulness and could work injustice on innocent third parties instead of protecting them.

The Report recommended that a company should enjoy all the powers of a natural person subject to any specific limits imposed on the powers of the company, in the company's articles of incorporation.

Barbados, the Bahamas and Guyana have adopted the recommend-ation. See, for example, section 17 of the Barbados Act which provides as follows:

17 (i) a company has the capacity and, subject to this Act, the rights, powers and privileges of an 'individual'.

Doctrine of Constructive Notice

The Report recommended also that the doctrine of constructive notice be abolished in the form that no one is to be deemed to have constructive notice of a company's documents by reason of the fact that they have been filed with the Registrar. This was adopted by Barbados, Bahamas and Guyana.

Limited Liability Clause

This clause in the memorandum merely states that the liability of the members is limited. In the case of a company limited by shares, the effect is that the liability of a member is limited to the amount if any unpaid on his shares. In the case a company limited by guarantee, the member's liability is limited to the amount that he undertakes to contribute to the assets of the company in the event of a winding-up.

Share Capital Clause

The share capital clause of the memorandum of a company limited by shares must state the amount of the share capital with which the company proposes to be registered and the division thereof into shares of a fixed amount. No subscriber may take less than one share.

See chapter 9 where this is dealt with separately.

The Association Clause

In this clause the subscribers to the memorandum declare that they desire to be formed into a company, in pursuance of the memorandum, and agree to take the number of shares set opposite their respective names.

Subscription Clause

The subscribers (at least two for a private company and seven for a public company) must, in their own handwriting, sign the memorandum, add their addresses and descriptions and state, against their names, the number of shares for which they subscribe. No subscriber may take less than one share.

The subscribers' signatures must be witnessed (it is the practice for one person to witness the signatures of all the subscribers).

A subscriber to the memorandum is deemed to have agreed to become a member of the company.

A minor, another company or a person resident abroad can be subscribers to the memorandum.

Alteration of the Memorandum of Association

Every clause of the memorandum may be altered except the registered office clause[7]. Such clauses can be altered by special resolution[8] unless the memorandum provides for another method. It is usually provided that holders of fifteen percent of the issued shares have twenty-one days to apply to the court to challenge the alteration.

The company must deliver a copy of the memorandum as altered to the Registrar of Companies for registration.

In the case of an alteration of the objects clause, it is normally provided that the company has the power to alter its objects clause at any time by special resolution for *certain specified purposes* only.

Once the special resolution is passed, the company must wait for a period, usually twenty-one days, to allow for an application to be made to the court to cancel the alteration. If there is no objection then the company must deliver to the Registrar a copy of the memorandum as altered for registration.

If an application is made to the court objecting to the alteration, the alteration is ineffective unless confirmed by the court.

Generally, the objector or objectors must have at least 15 percent of issued share capital.

As far as the objects clause is concerned this can only be altered for the following purposes:

(a) to carry on its business more economically or efficiently;
(b) to attain its main purpose by new or improved means;
(c) to enlarge or change the local area of operation;

(d)   to carry on some business which may be conveniently combined with its own;

(e)   to restrict or abandon any of its objects;

(f)   to sell or dispose of all or any of its undertaking; or

(g)   to amalgamate with another company.

Where an alteration is made to the memorandum, any copy issued after alteration must be in accordance with the alteration.

- **Example of a Memorandum of Association (for Jamaica) with an expanded objects clause**

THE COMPANIES ACT
MEMORANDUM OF ASSOCIATION OF   COMPANY LIMITED

I   The name of the company is   COMPANY LIMITED.

2   The Registered Office of the company will be situated at any place in the island of Jamaica that the directors may determine from time to time.

3   The objects for which the company is established are:

A   i   To carry on the business or businesses of proprietors and keepers of snack bars, luncheon counters, cafes, refreshment rooms, restaurants, hotels, inns, beer houses and tavern, and of licensed victuallers, wine and spirit merchants, distillers and brewers, importers, manufacturers of aerated and mineral waters and other drinks, provision dealers, cigar merchants and tobacconists, general storekeepers, and manufacturers' agents.

ii   To appropriate any part or parts of the property of the company for the purpose of and to build or let shops, offices, and other places of business and to use or lease any part of the property of the company not required for the purposes aforesaid for any purpose for which it may be conveniently used or let.

iii   To acquire and deal with any of the following properties

a   Lands, buildings, easements or other interests in real estate

b   Plant, machinery, personal estate and effects

c   Shares or stock or securities in or of the company, business or undertaking, the acquisition of which may promote or advance the interests of the company.

d   Patents, patent rights or investments, copyright designs, trade marks and secret processes.

e   The business, property and liabilities of any company, firm or person carrying on any business within the objects of the company.

B   To vary the investments of the company and to sell, let, rent, mortgage, charge, dispose of or otherwise deal with or grant rights over or any part of the property of the company PROVIDED ALWAYS that no surplus arising from such sale shall be available for distribution through the profit and loss account.

C   To erect and construct houses, buildings or works of every description on any land of the company, or upon any other lands or property, and to pull down, rebuild, enlarge, alter and improve existing houses, buildings or works thereon, to convert and appropriate any such land into and for roads, streets, squares, gardens and pleasure grounds and other conveniences, and generally to deal with and improve the property of the company.

D   To undertake or direct the management of the property, buildings, lands and estates (of any tenure or kind) of any persons, whether members of the company or not, in the capacity of stewards or receivers or otherwise.

E   To acquire whether by purchase, lease, exchange or otherwise, howsoever office, premises and accommodation for the purpose of leasing the same or making the same available to any person, firm or company.

F   To acquire whether by purchase, hire, exchange or otherwise howsoever office furniture and equipment of all kinds for the purpose of hiring the same or otherwise making the same available for use by any person, firm or company.

G   To engage or hire professional, clerical, manual and other staff and workers to enter into agreements with such staff and workers with a view to allocate their services to any person, firm or company requiring same.

H   To pay all the costs and expenses of the promotion and establish-ment of the company whether in cash or by the issue of fully or partly paid up shares or partly in one way and partly in the other.

J   To establish branches, agencies and/or sub-agents in Jamaica and elsewhere and to regulate and discontinue all or any of them.

K   To grant licences to use any patents or secret processes of the company.

L   To draw, make, accept, endorse, negotiate, discount, execute and issue all negotiable or transferrable instruments including bills of exchange, cheques, promissory notes, bills of lading, warrants, debentures, and all or any other kind of negotiable instruments.

M   To borrow money or to receive money on deposit either without security or secured by debenture, debenture stock (perpetual or terminable), mortgage or other security charged on the undertaking or on all or any of the assets of the company including uncalled capital.

N   To lend money with or without security and to invest money of the company in such manner, other than in the shares of the company, as the Directors may think fit.

O   To promote and establish companies, whether or not with objects similar to the company.

P   To provide for the welfare of persons employed or formerly employed by the company or any predecessors in business of the company and the wives, widows and families of such persons by grants of money or other aid or otherwise as the Directors may think fit.

Q   To subscribe or contribute to or otherwise aid benevolent, charitable, national or other institutions or objects whether of a private or of a public character or which have any moral or other claims to support or aid by the company by reason of the locality of their operation or otherwise.

R   To act as guarantor or surety and for either purpose to give security, as the Directors may think fit.

S   To promote any company or companies for the purpose of acquiring all or any of the property or liabilities of the company or for any other purpose of acquiring all or any of the property or liabilities of the company.

T   To do all or any of the above things in any part of the world as principals, agents, contractors, trustees or otherwise.

U   To distribute specie or shares the assets of the company amongst the members of the company in such manner and on such terms as the Directors may determine.

V   To do all or any of the things hereinbefore authorized either alone or in conjunction with or as factors, trustees or agents for others of by or through factors, trustees or agents.

W   To do all such things as are incidental or conducive to the attainment of the above objects or any of them.

4   The liability of the members is limited.

5   The share capital of the company is TWO THOUSAND DOLLARS ($2,000) divided into 1,000 shares of $2.00 each.

The shares in the original or in any increased capital may be divided into several classes, and there may be attached thereto respectively any preferential deferred or other special rights, privileges, conditions or restrictions as to dividend, capital voting or otherwise.

We, the several persons whose names and addresses are subscribed, are desirous of being formed into a company in pursuance of this

Memorandum of Association, and We respectively agree to take the number of shares in the capital of the company set opposite our respective names.

Names	Addresses	Description of Subscribers	No. of shares taken by each subscriber

DATED THIS   day of   19

WITNESS to the above signatures

Notice of Change of Name

X   **Company Limited**

CHANGE OF NAME

NOTICE
THE COMPANIES ACT,
SPECIAL RESOLUTION (Pursuant to Section   ) of **X** Company Limited, passed on the 7th June 199   .

At an EXTRAORDINARY GENERAL MEETING of the Members of the said company, duly convened and held at   on 7th June 199   , the following RESOLUTION was duly passed as a SPECIAL RESOLUTION:

RESOLUTION

"That with the consent of the Registrar of Companies, the name of the Company be changed to   LIMITED"

_____ Secretary

Notes

1. For Barbados only the "Articles of Incorporation" is required, Guyana has similar provisions as Barbados under the 1991 Act (not yet in force). See pp. 27-28, supra.
2. See p. 134, infra.
3. If the central control is in more than one place, then a company may have more than one residence.
4. Usually within 14 days of the change.
5. Except for Barbados, the Bahamas and Guyana under their recent legislations.
6. No longer so for Barbados and Bahamas. In these territories, a company has the capacity of an individual. see pp. 7-8, supra.
7. The Companies Act, 1862 (U.K.) permitted a company to change its name and its nominal capital only. Subsequent Acts extended the range of alterations that may be made.
8. See pp. 134-36, infra.

CHAPTER 6

The Articles
of Association

The Articles of Association of a registered company are the regulations dealing with the internal management of the company. The management of every registered company is governed by articles[1]. Detailed articles are provided for in Tables to be found in Schedules to the relevant Act. See, for example, Table A in the First Schedule. Table A[2] provides for a model set of Articles for a public or a private company limited by shares. It can be adopted, modified or rejected. It deals with a number of different internal matters including:

(a) Shares – *share capital, share certificates, lien, calls, transfers, alteration of share capital and variation of rights*

(b) Meetings – *general meetings, notice; proceedings, voting*

(c) Directors – *number, power, appointment, disqualification, removal, remuneration, meetings*

(d) Company Secretary

(e) Minutes

(f) The Company Seal

(g) Financial Matters – *dividends, accounts, capitalization of profits*

(h) Notices of Meetings

(i) Winding-up – *special provisions*

A company limited by shares need not register articles, though other types of companies are required to do so. If articles are not registered,

Table A automatically applies. Even if articles are registered, Table A still applies, unless it has been specifically excluded or modified.

Private companies normally adopt the majority of the articles in Table A excluding or modifying those which are unsuitable to the needs of the particular company. Public companies usually submit their own articles, inserting those in Table A which are relevant to its specific needs.

The articles must be signed by the subscribers to the memorandum and witnessed.

Alteration of Articles

Articles are normally altered by special resolution[3] at a general meeting of the company. Articles can also be altered by the *unanimous agreement of all the shareholders* whether or not they attend a meeting or pass a resolution. In *Cane* v *Jones* [1980] all the members agreed to change an article which gave the chairman a casting vote. They did not formally meet. Nevertheless, it was held that the article was validly changed.

A company can alter its articles even though the minority shareholders consider their interests to be prejudiced. There are certain rules to be borne in mind when altering the articles of a company, as the power to alter the articles places considerable power in the hands of the majority which, in some cases, can be one shareholder. Because of this, the court has found it necessary to control this power to amend the articles in the following ways:

(a) The articles are subject to the memorandum; if there is a conflict, the memorandum will prevail (see *Allen* v *Gold Reefs of West Africa Ltd.* [1900]).

(b) Any alteration must be lawful.

(c) An alteration must not increase the liability of a member without his consent.

(d) The alteration must be made bona fide for the benefit of the company as a whole (*Allen* v *Gold Reefs of West Africa Ltd.* [1900]).

(e) If the alteration involves a breach of contract, it will be valid in spite of the breach but an injured party will have the normal remedies available to him for the breach (*Southern Foundries* [1926] *Ltd.* v *Shirlaw* [1940] AC 701).

A copy of the special resolution altering the articles must be filed with the Registrar (usually within fifteen days) after the resolution was passed.

Bona fide for the Company as a Whole

The power to alter the articles must be exercised bona fide for the benefit of the company as a whole. The minority shareholders may seek to show that an alteration was not made bona fide for the benefit of the company as a whole. To do this, they will have to show either that the action of the majority was motivated by malice or that they were discriminated against by the majority. This places a heavy burden on a minority shareholder who seeks to oppose an alteration.

Malice is a desire to harm or injure a person by depriving him of his rights and a discriminatory act, is an act which benefits a section of the company without benefitting the company as a whole. In *Sidebottom* v *Kershaw Leese & Co.* [1920] 1 Ch 154 an alteration of the articles was approved although it provided for the compulsory purchase of shares from shareholders who carried on business in competition with the company. It was held that the alteration benefitted the company as a whole and was valid. Lord Sterndale M.R. said:

> "I think looking at the alteration broadly that it is for the benefit of the company that they should not be obliged to have amongst them as members persons who are competing with them in business and who may get knowledge from their membership which would enable them to compete better ..."

If a private company alters its articles so that it no longer includes the conditions required for a private company, the company ceases to be a private company and the company must deliver a prospectus or otherwise indicate to the Registrar within fourteen days.

Allen v *Gold Reefs of West Africa* [1900] 1 Ch 656 concerned an attempted alteration of the articles of association which would have retrospective effect and alter the obligations of a shareholder towards the company. The court held that, provided the alteration could be seen as bona fide for the benefit of the company, the power to alter the articles was otherwise unfettered.

Lindley M.R. said:

> "The power thus conferred on companies to alter the regulations contained in their articles is limited only by the provisions contained in the statues and the conditions contained in the company's memorandum of association. Wide, however, as the language of the Act is, the power conferred by it must, like all other powers, be exercised subject to those general principles of law and equity which are applicable to all powers conferred on majorities and enabling them to bind minorities. It must be exercised, not only in the manner required by law, but also bona fide for the benefit of the company as a whole, and it must not be exceeded."

In *Greenhalgh* v *Arderne Cinemas* [1951] Ch 286 Eveshed MR said:

> "Certain principles can be safely stated as emerging from [the] authorities. In the first place, I think it is now plain that 'bona fide for the benefit of the company as a whole' means not two things but one thing. It means the shareholder must proceed upon what in his honest opinion, is for the benefit of the company as a whole. The second thing is that the phrase 'the company as a whole' does not (at any rate in such a case as the present) mean the company as a commercial entity, distinct from the corporation as a general body. That is to say, the case may be taken of an individual hypothetical member and it may be asked whether what is proposed is, in the honest opinion of those who voted in its favour, for that person's benefit.

> I think that the matter can, in practice be more accurately and precisely stated by looking at the converse and by saying that a special resolution of this kind would be liable to be impeached if the effect of it were to discriminate between the majority shareholders and the minority shareholders, so as to give the former an advantage of which the latter were deprived . . ."

The cases show a reluctance on the part of the courts to intervene. In the *Greenhalgh* case, a change in Articles which removed the plaintiff's pre-emption rights was approved.

In *Rights and Issue Investment Trust Ltd.* v *Stylo Shoes Ltd.* [1965] Ch 250 the alteration halves the voting rights of a number of shareholders as against the rights by management. Despite this, the resolution was upheld.

In all these cases, it is the company as a separate person whose benefit is to be considered. The rule that a company can alter its articles even to the disadvantage of some of its members is however subject to exceptions. First, the alteration must not amount to minority oppression[4]. Secondly, a company cannot, by an alteration of its articles deprive a member of vested rights. Thirdly, if the company commits a breach of contract by altering the articles it will be liable in damages.

The Legal Effect of Articles (and Memorandum)

The articles (together with the memorandum) bind the company and the members as though signed and sealed by each member. The effect is that the company is bound contractually to the members and the members to each other. The articles and memorandum contain the terms of the contract. The company and the members are the parties to the contract. A member, however, can only enforce the articles in the capacity as a member and not as an outsider.

In *Eley* v *Positive Government Security Life Assurance Co. Ltd.* [1876] the articles provided that Eley should be employed for life as a solicitor to the company. The company ceased to employ him as a solicitor and he sued for breach of contract. It was held that he could not rely on the Articles as it was a contract between the members and the company and he was not seeking to enforce his right as a member but as a solicitor.

In *Pender* v *Lushington* [1877], the company's articles provided that a member was not entitled to cast more than one hundred votes. The plaintiff transferred shares to nominees to circumvent this provision. The chairman refused to accept the votes cast by the nominees. It was held that the company was contractually bound by the articles to recognize the votes of members and the nominees were members.

In *Wood* v *Odessa Waterworks Co.* (1889) a company proposed to pay a dividend by issuing debentures instead of paying by cash as provided by the articles. The company was prevented from doing as proposed as this was a breach of the articles.

In commenting on the decision Sterling J. said:

> "The articles of association constitute a contract not merely between the share-holders and the company, but between each individual shareholder and every other."

The contract formed by the articles of association is an unusual one, in that its terms may be altered from time to time by a three-quarters majority of the members against the wishes of the minority of members (i.e. by special resolution).

No member shall be bound by an alteration made to the memorandum or to the articles after the date he becomes a member, if the alteration requires him to take more shares or increases his liability to the company .

Copies of the memorandum and articles are usually required to be given to members on payment of a prescribed fee.

Notification of Alteration

Any alteration of the articles must be notified to the Registrar usually within fifteen days of the alteration.

- **SPECIMEN TABLE A**
  (contained in the BELIZE COMPANIES ACT[5])

TABLE A
Regulations for Management of a Company Limited by Shares

PRELIMINARY

I   In these regulations, unless the context otherwise required, expression defined in the Companies Ordinance, or any statutory modification thereof in force at the date at which these regulations become binding on the company, shall have the meanings so defined; and words importing the singular shall include the plural, and vice versa, and words importing the masculine gender shall include females, and works importing persons shall include bodies corporate.

BUSINESS

2   The directors shall have regard to the restrictions on the commencement of business imposed by section 87 of the Companies Ordinance, if, and so far as, those restrictions are binding upon the company.

SHARES

3   Subject to the provisions, if any, in that behalf of the memorandum of association of the company, and without prejudice to any special rights previously conferred on the holders of existing shares in the company,

any share in the company may be issued with such preferred, deferred, or other special rights, or such restrictions, whether in regard to dividend, voting, return of share capital, or otherwise, as the company may from time to time by special resolution determine.

4   If at any time the share capital is divided into different classes of shares, the rights attached to any class (unless otherwise provided by the terms of issue of the shares of that class) may be varied with the consent in writing of the holders of three-fourths of the issued shares of that class or with the sanction of any extraordinary resolution passed at a separate general meeting of the holders of the shares of the class. To every such general meetings shall mutatis mutandis apply, but so that the necessary quorum shall be two persons at least holding or representing by proxy one-third of the issued shares of the class.

5   No share shall be offered to the public for subscription except upon the terms that the amount payable on application shall be at least five per cent of the nominal amount of the share; and the directors shall, as regards any allotment of shares, duly comply with such of the provisions by sections 85 and 88 of the Companies Ordinance, as may be applicable thereto.

6   Every person whose name is entered as a member in the register of members shall, without payment, be entitled to a certificate under the common seal of the company specifying the share or share s held by him and the amount paid up thereon, provided that in respect of a share or shares held jointly by several persons the company shall not be bound to issue more than one certificate, and delivery of a certificate for a share to one of several joint holders shall be sufficient delivery to all.

7   If a share certificate is defaced, lost, or destroyed, it may be renewed on payment of such fee, if any, not exceeding twenty-five cents, and on such terms, if any, as to evidence and indemnity as the directors think fit.

8   No part of the funds of the company shall be employed in the purchase of or in loans upon the security of the company's shares.

LIEN

9   The company shall have a lien on every share (not being a fully-paid share) for all moneys (whether presently payable or not) called or payable at a fixed time in respect of that share, and the company shall also have the name of a single persons, for all moneys presently payable by him or his estate to the company; but the directors may at any time declare any share to be wholly or in part exempt from the provisions of this clause. The company's lien, if any, on a share shall extend to all dividends payable thereon.

10   The company may sell, in such manner as the directors think fit, any shares on which the company has a lien, but no sale shall be made unless one sum in respect of which the lien exists, is presently payable nor until the expiration of fourteen days after a notice in writing, stating and demanding payment of such part of the amount in respect of which the lien exists as is presently payable, has been given to the registered holder for the time being of the share or the person entitled by reason of his death or bankruptcy to the share.

11   The proceeds of the sale shall be applied in payment of such part of the amount in respect of which the lien exists as is presently payable, and the residue shall (subject to a like lien of sums not presently payable as existed upon the shares prior to the sale) be paid to the person entitled to the shares at the date of the sale. The purchaser shall be registered as the holder of the shares, and he shall not be bound to see to the application of the purchase money, nor shall his title to the shares be affected by any irregularity or invalidity in the proceedings in reference to the sale.

CALLS ON SHARES

12   The directors may from time to time make calls upon the members in respect of any moneys unpaid on their shares, provided that no call shall exceed one-fourth of the nominal amount of the share, or be payable at less than one month from the last call; and each member shall (subject to receiving at least fourteen days' notice specifying the time or times of payment) pay to the company at the time or times so specified the amount called on his shares.

13   The joint holders of a share shall be jointly and severally liable to pay all calls in respect thereof.

14   If a sum called in respect of a share is not paid before or on the day appointed for payment thereof, the person from whom the sum is due shall pay interest upon the sum at the rate of five dollars per centum per annum from the day of the appointed payment thereof to the time of the actual payment; but the directors shall be at liberty to waive payment of that interest wholly or in part.

15   The provisions of these regulations as to payment of interest shall apply in the case of non-payment of any sum which, by the terms of issue of a share, becomes payable at a fixed time, whether on account of the amount of the share, or by way of premium, as if the same had become payable by virtue of a call duly made and notified.

16   The directors may make arrangements on the issue of shares for a difference between the holders in the amount of calls to be paid and in the times of payment.

17 The directors may, if they think fit, receive from any member willing to advance the same, all or any part of the moneys uncalled and unpaid upon any shares held by him and upon all or any of the moneys so advanced may (until the same would, but for such advance, become presently payable) pay interest at such rate (not exceeding, without the sanction of the company in general meeting, six per centum), as may be agreed upon between the member payment sum in advance and the directors.

TRANSFER AND TRANSMISSION OF SHARES

18 The instrument of transfer of any share in the company shall be executed both by the transferor and transferee, and the transferor shall be deemed to remain a holder of the share until the name of the transferee is entered in the register of members in respect thereof.

19 Shares in the company shall be transferred in the following form, or in any usual or common form which the directors shall approve:

I, A.B. of   in consideration of \$ paid to me by C.D., of   (hereinafter called "the said transferee"), do hereby transfer to the said transferee the shares [or shares] numbered   in the undertaking called the Company, Limited, to hold unto the said transferee, his executors, administrators, and assigns, subject to the several conditions on which I held the same at the time of the executor thereof; and I, the said transferee, do hereby agree to take the said share [or shares] subject to the conditions aforesaid. As witness our hands the day of

WITNESS TO THE SIGNATURES OF, ETC.

20 The directors may decline to register any transfer of shares, not being fully-paid shares, to a person of whom they do not approve, and may also decline to register any transfer of shares on which the company has a lien. The directors may also suspend the registration of transfers during the fourteen days immediately preceding the ordinary general meeting in each year. The directors may decline to recognise any instrument of transfer unless:

a a fee not exceeding seventy-five cents is paid to the company in respect thereof, and

b the instrument of transfer is accompanied by the certificate of the shares to which it relates, and such other evidence as the directors may reasonably require to show the right of the transferor to make the transfer.

21 The executors or administrators of a deceased sole holder of a share shall be the only persons recognised by the company as having any title to the share. In the case of a share registered in the names of two or more holders, the survivors or survivor, or the executors or administrators of the deceased survivor, shall be the only persons recognised by the company as having any title to the share.

22 Any person becoming entitled to a share in consequence of the death or bankruptcy of a member shall, upon such evidence being produced as may from time to time be required by the directors, have the right either be the registered himself, to make such transfer of the share as the deceased or bankrupt person could have made; but the directors shall, in either case, have the same right to decline or suspend registration as they would have had in the case of a transfer of the share by the deceased or bankrupt person before the death or bankruptcy.

23 A person becoming entitled to a share by reason of the death or bankruptcy of the holder shall be entitled to the same dividends and other advantages to which he would be entitled if he were the registered holder of the share, except that he shall not, before being registered as a member in respect of the share, be entitled in respect of it to exercise any right conferred by membership in relation to meetings of the company.

FORFEITURE OF SHARES

24 If a member fails to pay any call or instalment of a call on the day appointed for payment thereof, the directors may, at any time thereafter during such time as any part of such call or instalment remains unpaid, serve a notice on him requiring payment of so much of the call or instalment as is unpaid, together with any interest which may have accrued.

25 The notice shall name a further day (not earlier than the expiration of fourteen days from the date of the notice) on or before which the payment required by the notice is to be made, shall state that in the event of non-payment or before the time appointed the shares in respect of which the call was made will be liable to be forfeited.

26 If the requirements of any such notice as aforesaid are not accompanied with, any share in respect of which the notice has been given may at any time thereafter, before the payment required by the notice has been made, be forfeited by a resolution of the directors to that effect.

27 A forfeited share may be sold or otherwise disposed of on such terms and in such manner as the directors think fit, but shall, notwithstanding, remain liable to pay to the company all moneys which, at the date of forfeiture, were presently payable by him to the company in respect of

the shares, but his liability shall cease if and when the company receive payment in fill of the nominal amount of the shares.

28 A person whose shares have been forfeited shall cease to be a member in respect of the forfeited shares, but shall, notwithstanding, remain liable to pay to the company all moneys which, at the date of forfeiture, were presently payable by him to the company in respect of the shares, but his liability shall cease if and when the company receive payment in full of the nominal amount of the shares.

29 A statutory declaration in writing that the declarant is a director of the company, and that a share in the company has been duly forfeited on a date stated in the declaration, shall be conclusive evidence of the facts therein stated as against all persons claiming to be entitled to the share, and that declaration, and the receipt of the company for the consideration, if any, given for the share on the sale or disposition thereof shall constitute a good title to the share, and the person to whom the share is sold or disposed of shall be registered as the holder of the share and shall not be bound to see to the application of the purchase money, if any, nor shall his title to the share be affected by any irregularity or invalidity in the proceedings in reference to the forfeiture, sale or disposal of the share.

30 The provisions of these regulations as to forfeiture shall apply in the case of non-payment of any sum which, by the terms of issue of a share, becomes payable at a fixed time, whether on account of the amount of the share, or by way of premium, as if the same had been payable by virtue of a call duly made and notified.

CONVERSION OF SHARES INTO STOCK

31 The directors may, with the sanction of the company previously given in general meeting, convert any paid-up shares into stock, and may with the like sanction reconvert any stock into paid-up shares of any denomination.

32 The holders of stock may transfer the same, or any part thereof, in the same manner, and subject to the same regulations, as, and subject to which, the shares from which the stock arose might previously to conversion have been transferred, or as near thereto as circumstance admit; but the directors may from time to time fix the minimum amount of stock transferable, and restrict or forbid the transfer of fractions of that minimum, but the minimum shall not exceed the nominal amount of the shares from which the stock arose.

33 The holders of stock shall, according to the amount of the stock held by them, have the same rights, privileges and advantages as regards

dividends, voting at meetings of the company, and other matters as if they held the shares from which the stock arose, but no such privilege or advantage (except participation in the dividends and profits of the company) shall be conferred by any such aliquot part of stock as would not, if existing in shares, have conferred that privilege or advantage.

34   Such of the regulations of the company (other than those relating to share warrants) as are applicable to paid-up shares shall apply to stock, and the words "share" and "shareholder" therein shall include "stock" and "stock-holder".

SHARE WARRANTS

35   The company may issue share warrants, and accordingly the directors may in their discretion, with respect to any share which is fully paid up, on application in writing signed by the person registered holder of the share, and authenticated by such evidence, if any, as directors may from time to time require as to the identity of the person signing the request, and on receiving the certificate, if any, of the share and the amount of the stamp duty on the warrant and such fee as the directors may from time to time require, issue under the company's seal a warrant, duly stamped, stating that the bearer of the warrant is entitled to the shares therein specified, and may provide by coupons, or otherwise for the payment of dividends, or other moneys, on the shares included in the warrant.

36   A share warrant shall entitle the bearer to the shares included in it, and the shares shall be transferred by the delivery of the share warrant, and the provisions of the regulations of the company with respect to the transfer and transmission of shares shall not apply thereto.

37   The bearer of a share warrant shall, on surrender of the warrant to the company for cancellation, and on payment of such sum as the directors may from time to time prescribe, be entitled to have his name entered as a member in the register of members in respect of the shares included in the warrant.

38   The bearer of a share warrant may at any time deposit the warrant at the office of the company, and so long as the warrant remains so deposited the depositor shall have the same right of signing a requisition for calling a meeting of the company, and of attending and voting and exercising the other privileges of a member at any meeting held after the expiration of two clear days from the time of deposit, as if his name were inserted in the register of members as the holder of the shares included in the deposit warrant. Not more than one person shall be recognised as depositor of the share warrant. The company shall, on two days' written notice, return the deposited share warrant to the depositor.

39 Subject herein otherwise expressly provided, no person shall, as bearer of a share warrant, sign a requisition for calling a meeting of the company, or attend, or vote, or exercise any other privilege of a member at a meeting of the company, or be entitled to receive any notices from the company; but the bearer of a share warrant shall be entitled in all other respects to the same privileges and advantages as if he were named in the register of members as the holer of the shares included in the warrant, and he shall be a member of the company.

40 The directors may from time to time make rules as to the terms on which (if they shall think fit) a new share warrant or coupon may be issued by way of renewal in case of defacement, loss or destruction.

ALTERATION OF CAPITAL

41 The directors may, with the sanction of any extraordinary resolution of the company, increase the share capital by such sum to be divided into shares of such amount, as the resolution shall prescribe.

42 (1) Subject to any direction to the contrary that may be given by the resolution sanctioning the increase of share capital, all new shares shall, before issue, be offered to such persons as at the date of the offer are entitled to receive notices from the company of general meetings in proportion, as nearly as the circumstances admit, to the amount of the existing shares to which they are entitled.

(2) The offer shall be made by notice specifying the number of shares offered, and limiting a time within which the offer, if not accepted, will be deemed to be declined, and, after the expiration of that time, or on the receipt of an intimation from the person to whom the offer is made that he declines to accept the shares offered, the directors may dispose of the same in such manner as they think most beneficial to the company. The directors may likewise so dispose of any new shares which (by reason of the ratio which the new shares bear to shares held by persons entitled to an offer of new shares) cannot, in the opinion of the directors, be conveniently offered under this article.

43 The new shares shall be subject to the same provisions with reference to the payment of calls, lien, transfer, transmission, forfeiture, and otherwise as the shares in the original share capital.

44 The company may, by special resolution:
a   consolidate and divide its share capital into shares of larger amounts than its existing shares;
b   by subdivision of its existing shares, or any of them, divide the whole, or any part of its share capital into shares of smaller

amount than is fixed by the memorandum of association, subject, nevertheless, to the provisions of paragraph (d) of subsection (1) of section 41 of the Companies Ordinance.

c   cancel any shares which, at the date of the passing of the resolution, have not been taken or agreed to be taken by any person;

d   reduce its share capital in any manner and with, and subject to, any incident authorized, and consent required by law.

GENERAL MEETINGS

45   The statutory general meeting of the company shall be held within the period required by section 65 of the Companies Ordinance.

46   A general meeting shall be held once in every year at such time (not being more than fifteen months after the holding of the last preceding general meeting) and place as may be prescribed by the company in general meeting, or in default, at such time in the month following that in which the anniversary of the company's incorporation occurs, and at such place, as the directors shall appoint. In default of a general meeting being so held, a general meeting shall be held in the month next following, and may be convened by any two members in the same manner as nearly as possible as that in which meetings are to be convened by the directors.

47   The above-mentioned general meetings shall be called ordinary meetings; all other general meetings shall be called extraordinary.

48   (1) The directors may, whenever they think fit, convene an extraordinary general meeting, and extraordinary general meetings shall also be convened on such requisition, or, in default, may be convened by such requisitionists, as provided by section 66 of the Companies Ordinance.

(2) If at any time there are not within Belize sufficient directors capable of acting to form a quorum, any director or any two members of the company may convene an extraordinary general meeting in the same manner as nearly as possible as that in which meetings may be convened by the directors.

PROCEEDINGS AT GENERAL MEETING

49   Seven days' notice at the least (exclusive of the day on which the notice is served or deemed to be served, but inclusive of the day for which notice is given) specifying the place, the day, and the hour of meeting and, in case of special business, the general nature of that business shall be given in manner hereinafter mentioned, or in such other manner, if any, as may be prescribed by the company in general meeting, to such persons as are,

under the regulations of the company, entitled to receive such notices from the company; but the non-receipt of the notice by any member shall not invalidate the proceedings at any general meeting.

50 All business shall be deemed special that is transacted at any extra-ordinary meeting, and all that is transacted at an ordinary meeting, with the exception of sanctioning a dividend, the consideration of the accounts, balance-sheets, and the ordinary report of the directors and auditors, the election of directors and other officers in the place of those retiring by rotation, and the fixing of the remuneration of the auditors.

51 No business shall be transacted at any general meeting unless a quorum of members is present at the time when the meeting proceeds to business; save as herein otherwise provided, their members personally present shall be a quorum.

52 If within half an hour from the time appointed for the meeting a quorum is not present, the meeting, if convened upon the requisition of members, shall be dissolved; in any other case it shall stand adjourned to the same day in the next week, at the same time and place, and, if at the adjourned meeting a quorum is not present within half an hour from the time appointed for the meeting the members present shall be a quorum.

53 The chairman, if any, of the board of directors, shall preside as chairman at every general meeting of the company.

54 If there is no such chairman, or if at any meeting he is not present within fifteen minutes after the time appointed for holding the meeting or is unwilling to act as chairman, the members present shall choose some one of their number to be chairman.

55 The chairman may, with the consent of any meeting at which a quorum is present (and shall if so directed by the meeting), adjourn the meeting from time to time and from place to place, but no business shall be transacted at any adjourned meeting other than the business left unfinished at the meeting from which the adjournment took place. When a meeting is adjourned for ten days or more, notice of the adjourned meeting shall be given as in the case of an original meeting. Save as aforesaid it shall not be necessary to give any notice of an adjournment or of the business to be transacted at an adjourned meeting.

56 At any general meeting a resolution put to the vote of the meeting shall be decided on a show of hands, unless a poll is (before or on the declaration of the result of the show of hands) demanded by at least three members, and, unless a poll is so demanded, a declaration by the chairman that a resolution has, on a show of hands been carried, or carried unanimously, or by a particular majority, or lost, and an entry to that effect in the book of the proceedings of the company shall be

conclusive evidence of the fact, without proof of the number or proportion of the votes recorded in favour of, or against, that resolution.

57   If a poll is duly demanded it shall be taken in such manner as the chairman directs, and the result of the poll shall be deemed to be the resolution of the meeting at which the poll was demanded.

58   In the case of an equality of votes, whether on a show of hands or on a poll, the chairman of the meeting at which the show of hands takes place or at which the poll is demanded, shall be entitled to a second or casting vote.

59   A poll demanded on the election of a chairman, or on a question of adjournment, shall be taken forthwith. A poll demanded on any other question shall be taken as such time as the chairman of the meeting directs.

VOTES OF MEMBERS

60   On a show of hands, every member present in person shall have one vote. On a poll every member shall have one vote for each share of which he is the holder.

61   In the case of joint holders the vote of the senior who tenders a vote, whether in person or by proxy, shall be accepted to the exclusion of the votes of the other joint holders; and for this purpose seniority shall be determined by the order in which the names stand in the register of members.

62   A member of unsound mined, or in respect of whom an order has been made by any court having jurisdiction in lunacy, may vote, whether on a show of hands or on a poll, by his committee, curator bonis, or whether person in the nature of a committee or curator bonis appointed by that court, and any such committee, curator bonis, or other person may, on a poll, vote by proxy.

63   No member shall be entitled to vote at any general meeting unless all calls or other sums presently payable by him in respect of shares in the company have been paid.

64   On a poll votes may be given either personally or by proxy.

65   The instrument appointing a proxy shall be in writing under the hand of the appointor or of his attorney duly authorized in writing, or, if the appointor is a corporation, either under the common seal, or under the hand of an officer or attorney so authorized. No person shall act as a proxy unless either he is entitled on his own behalf to be present and vote at the meeting at which he acts as proxy, or he has been appointed to act at that meeting as proxy for a corporation.

66   The instrument appointing a proxy and the power of attorney or other

authority, if any, under which it is signed or a notarially certified copy of that power or authority shall be deposited at the registered office of the company not less than forty-eight hours before the time for holding the meeting at which the person named in the instrument proposes to vote, and in default the instrument of proxy shall not be treated as valid.

67   An instrument appointing a proxy may be in the following form, or in any other form which the directors shall approve:

Company, Limited.

"I   of   in the district of being a member of the   Company, Limited, hereby appoint   of   as my proxy to vote for me and on my behalf at the [ordinary or extraordinary as the case may be] general meeting of the company to be held on the   day of and at any adjournment thereof."

Directors.

68   The number of the directors and the names of the first directors shall be determined in writing by a majority of the subscribers of the memorandum of association.

69   The remuneration of the directors shall from time to time be determined by the company in general meeting.

70   The qualification of a director shall be the holding of at least one share in the company, and it shall be his duty to comply with the provisions of section 73 of the Companies Ordinance.

POWERS AND DUTIES OF DIRECTORS

71   The business of the company shall be managed by the directors who may pay all expense incurred in getting up and registering the company, and may exercise all such powers of the company as are not, by the Companies Ordinance, or any statutory modification thereof for the time being in force, or by these articles, required to be exercised by the company in general meeting, subject nevertheless to any regulation of these articles, to the provisions of the said Ordinance, and to such regulations, being not inconsistent with the aforesaid regulations or provisions, as may be prescribed by the company in general meeting; but no regulation made by the company in general meeting shall invalidate any prior act of the directors which would have been valid if that regulation had not been made.

72   The directors may from time to time appoint one or more of their body to the office of managing director or manager for such term, and at such remuneration (whether by way of salary, commission, or participation in profits, or partly in one way and partly in another) as they may think fit,

and a director so appointed shall not, while holding that office, be subject to retirement by rotation, or taken into account in determining the rotation of retirement of directors; but his appointment shall be subject to determination ipso factor if he ceases from any cause to be a director, or if the company in general meeting resolve that his tenure of the office of managing director or manager be determined.

73   The amount for the time being remaining undischarged of moneys borrowed or raised by the directors for the purposes of the company (otherwise than by the issue of share capital) shall not at any time exceed the issued share capital of the company without the sanction of the company in general meeting.

74   The directors shall cause minutes to be made in books provided for the purpose of:

a   all appointments of officers made by the directors;

b   the names of the directors present at each meeting of the directors and of any committee of the directors;

c   all resolutions and proceedings at all meetings of the company, and of the directors, and of committees of directors,

and every director present at any meeting of directors or committee of directors shall sign his name in a book to be kept for that purpose.

THE SEAL

76   The seal of the company shall not be affixed to any instrument except by the authority of a resolution of the Board of Directors, and in the presence of at least two directors and of the secretary or such other person as the directors may appoint for the purpose; and those two directors and secretary or other person as aforesaid shall sign every instrument to which the seal of the company is so affixed in their presence.

DISQUALIFICATIONS OF DIRECTORS

77   The office of director shall be vacated, if the director:

a   ceases to be a director by virtue of section 73 of the Companies Ordinance; or

b   holds any other office of profit under the company except that of managing director or manager; or

c   becomes bankrupt; or

d   is found a lunatic or becomes of unsound mind; or

e   is concerned or participates in the profits of any contract with the company:

Provided, however, that no director shall vacate his office by reason of his being a member of any company which has entered into contracts with or done any work for the company of which he is director; but a director shall not vote in respect of any such contract or work, and if he does so vote his vote shall not be counted.

ROTATION OF DIRECTORS

78 At the first ordinary meeting of the company the whole of the directors shall retire from office, and at the ordinary meeting in every subsequent year one-third of the directors for the time being, or, if their number is not three or a multiple of three, then the number nearest to one-third, shall retire from office.

79 The directors to retire every year shall be those who have been longest in office since their last election, but as between persons who became directors on the same day those to retire shall unless they otherwise agree among themselves be determined by lot.

80 A retiring director shall be eligible for re-election.

81 The company at the general meeting at which a director retires in manner aforesaid may fill the vacated office by electing a person thereto.

82 If at any meeting at which an election of directors ought to take place the places of the vacating directors are filled, the meeting shall stand adjourned till the same day in the next week at the same time and place, and, if at the adjourned meeting the places of the vacating directors are not filled, the vacating directors are filled, the vacating directors, or such of them as have not had their places filled, shall be deemed to have been re-elected at the adjourned meeting.

83 The company may from time to time in general meeting increase or reduce the number of directors, and may also determine in what rotation the increase or reduced number is to go out of office.

84 Any casual vacancy occurring in the board of directors may be filled up by the directors, but the person so chosen shall be subject to retirement at the same time as if he had become a director on the day on which the director in whose place he is appointed was last elected a director.

85 The directors shall have power at any time, and from time to time, to appoint a person as an additional director who shall retire from office at the next following ordinary general meeting, but shall be eligible for election by the company at that meeting as an additional director.

86 The company may by ordinary resolution remove any director before the expiration of his period of office, and may by an ordinary resolution appoint another person in his stead; the person so appointed shall be subject to retirement at the same time as if he had become a director on the day on which the director in whose place he is appointed was last elected a director.

PROCEEDINGS OF DIRECTORS

87 The directors may meet together for the despatch of business, adjourn, and otherwise regulate their meetings, as they think fit. Questions arising at any meeting shall be decided by a majority of votes. In case of an equality of votes the chairman shall have a second or casting vote. A director may, and the secretary on the requisition of a director shall, at any time summon a meeting of the directors.

88 The quorum necessary for the transaction of the business of the directors may be fixed by the directors, and unless so fixed shall (when the number of directors exceeds three) be three.

89 The continuing directors may notwithstanding any vacancy in their body, but, if and so long as their number is reduced below the number fixed by or pursuant to the regulations of the company as the necessary quorum of directors, the continuing directors may act for the purpose of increasing the number of directors to that number, or of summoning a general meeting of the company, but for no other purpose.

90 The directors may elect a chairman of their meetings and determine the period for which he is to hold office; but if no such chairman is elected, or if at any meeting the chairman is not present within five minutes after the time appointed for holding the same, the directors present may choose one of their number to be chairman of the meeting.

91 The directors may delegate any of their powers to committees consisting of such member or members of their body as they think fit; any committee so formed shall in the exercise of the powers so delegated conform to any regulations that may be imposed on them by the directors.

92 A committee may elect a chairman of their meetings; if no such chairman is elected, or if at any meeting the chairman is not present within five minutes after the time appointed for holding the same, the members present may choose one of their number to be chairman of the meeting.

93 A committee may meet and adjourn as they think proper. Questions arising at any meeting shall be determined by a majority of votes of the members present, and in case of any equality of votes the chairman shall have a second or casting vote.

94 All acts done by any number of the directors or of a committee of directors, or by any person acting as a director shall, notwithstanding that it be afterwards discovered that there was some defect in the appointment of any such directors or persons acting as aforesaid, or that they or any of them were disqualified, be as valid as if every such person had been duly appointed and was qualified to be a director.

DIVIDENDS AND RESERVE

95 The company in general meeting may declare dividends, but no dividend shall exceed the amount recommended by the directors.

96 The directors may from time to time pay to the members such interim dividends as appear to the directors to be justified by the profits of the company.

97 No dividend shall be paid otherwise than out of profits.

98 Subject to the rights of persons, if any, entitled to shares with special rights as to dividends, all dividends shall be declared and paid according to the amounts paid on the shares, but if and so long as nothing is paid up on any of the shares in the company, dividends may be declared and paid according to the amounts of the shares. No amount paid on a share in advance of calls shall, while carrying interest, be treated for purposes of this article as paid on the share.

99 The directors may, before recommending any dividend, set aside out of the profits of the company such sums as they think fit and a proper as a reserve or reserves which shall, at the discretion of the directors, be applicable for meeting contingencies, or for equalizing dividends, or for any other purpose to which the profits of the company may be properly applied, and pending such application may, at the like discretion, either be employed in the business of the company or be invested in such investments (other than shares of the company) as the directors may from time to time think fit.

100 If several persons are registered as joint holders of the share any one of them may give effectual receipt for any dividend payable on the share.

101 Notice of any dividend that may have been declared shall be given in manner hereinafter mentioned to the persons entitled to share therein.

102 No dividend shall bear interest against the company.

ACCOUNTS

103 The directors shall cause true accounts to be kept with respect to:

a all sums of money received and expended by the company and the matter in respect of which such receipts and expenditure takes place; and

b the assets and liabilities of the company.

104 The books of account shall be kept at the registered office of the company, or at such other place or places as the directors think fit, and shall always be open to the inspection of the directors.

105 The directors shall from time to time determine whether and to what extent and at what times and places and under what conditions or

regulations and accounts and books of the company or any of them shall be open to the inspection of members not being directors, and no member (not being a director) shall have any right of inspecting any account or book or document of the company, except as conferred by law or authorised by the directors or by the company in general meeting.

106 Once at least in every year, the directors shall lay before the company in general meeting a profit and loss account for the period since the preceding account or (in the case of the first account) since the incorporation of the company, made up to the date not more than six months before such meeting.

107 A balance sheet shall be made out in every year and laid before the company in general meeting made up to a date not more than six months before such meeting. The balance sheet shall be accompanied by a report of the directors as to the state of the company's affairs, and the amount which they recommend to be paid by way of dividend, and the amount, if any, which they propose to carry to a reserve fund.

108 A copy of the balance sheet and report shall, seven days previously to the meeting, be sent to the persons entitled to receive notices of general meetings in the manner in which notices are to be given hereunder.

109 Auditors shall be appointed and their duties regulated in accordance with sections 111 and 112 of the Companies Ordinance, or any statutory modification thereof for the time being in force.

NOTICE

110 (1) A notice may be given by the company to any member either personally or by sending it by post to him to his registered address, or (if he has no registered address in Belize) to the address, if any, within Belize supplied by him to the company for the giving of notices to him.
(2) Where a notice is sent by post, service of the notice shall be deemed to be effected by properly addressing, prepaying, and posting a letter containing the notice, and unless the contrary is proved to have been effected at the time at which the letter would be delivered in the ordinary course of post.

111 If a member has no registered address in Belize and has not supplied to the company an address within Belize for the giving of notices to him, a notice addressed to him and advertised in a newspaper circulating in the neighbourhood of the registered office of the company, shall be deemed to be duly given to him on the day on which the advertisement appears.

112 A notice may be given by the company to the joint holders of a share being giving notice to the joint holder named first in the register in respect of the share.

113 A notice may be given by the company to the persons entitled to a share in consequence of the death or bankruptcy of a member by sending it through the post in a prepaid letter addressed to them by name, or by the title of representatives of the deceased, or trustee of the bankrupt, or by any like description, at the address, if any, in Belize supplied for the purpose by the persons claiming to be so entitled, or (until such an address has been so supplied) by giving the notice in any manner in which the same might have been given if the death or bankruptcy had not occurred.

114 (1) Notice of every general meeting shall be given in some manner hereinbefore authorized to:

a   every member of the company (including bearer of share warrants) except those members who (having no registered address within Belize) have not supplied to the company an address within Belize for the giving of notices to them, and

b   every person entitled to a share in consequence of the death or bankruptcy of a member, who, but of notices or bankruptcy, would be entitled to receive notice of the meeting.

(2) No other persons shall be entitled to receive notices of general meetings.

Names	Addresses	Description of Subscribers	No. of shares taken by each subscriber

DATED THE   day of   199

WITNESS to the above signatures

Notes

1   For Barbados, only "Articles of Incorporation" are required to be registered; see p. 27, supra.
Instead of articles, a company may have a set of bye-laws regulating the conduct of the affairs of the company. For a model set of by-laws, see the Fourth Schedule of the Companies Regulation, 1984 (Barbados).

2.   See specimen Table A, p. 54, infra.

3.   See p. 34, supra.

4.   Where the alteration amounts to minority oppression, the remedies available under this heading should be sought. See chapter 16, p. 145, infra.

5.   This should be compared with Table A in the Jamaica Companies Act which is more elaborate.

CHAPTER 7

$\mathcal{P}$romotion
of $\mathcal{C}$ompanies

Promoters

Prior to its incorporation, a company has no legal existence. A company cannot form itself. Someone must promote it. The promoters of a company are those who are responsible for and take preparatory steps for its formation. Generally promoters are the persons who comply with the necessary formalities to register a company.

The promoters decide the activities of the proposed company; they decide whether to purchase an existing business; they would instruct an attorney-at-law to prepare the documents; they appoint the first directors; they provide the funds for registration and stamping of the documents.

A person who assists in the promotion of a company and acts in a professional capacity, e.g. a lawyer or an accountant, is not a promoter. A promoter may be a big businessman or small trader.

In *Twycross* v *Grant* [1877] 2 CPD 469, Cockburn CJ said:

"A promoter, I apprehend, is one who undertakes to form a company with reference to a given project and to set it going and who takes the necessary steps to accomplish that purpose. That the defendants were promoters of the company from the beginning can admit of no doubt. They framed the scheme; they not only provisionally framed the company but were, in fact to the end its creators, they found the directors and qualified them, they prepared the prospectus; they paid for printing and advertising and the expenses incidental to bring the undertaking before the world. In all these respects, the directors were passive; without saying that they were in a legal sense the agents of the defendants, they were certainly their instruments."

A person may become a promoter *after* the company is incorporated, e.g. if he raises capital for the newly formed company.

Duties of Promoters

Promoters are not agents or trustees of the company. A company cannot have an agent before incorporation as it has no legal personality until incorporation.

Because of the possibility of abuse, the courts have held that promoters stand in a fiduciary relationship with the company they are forming. They are in a position of trust and as such must act in good faith. This means that a promoter must not make secret profits. Any profits made from the promotion must be disclosed to the company, otherwise such profits may be recovered by the company when formed or the company may repudiate the transaction entered on its behalf or may obtain a court order for its rescission.

In *Erlanger v New Sombrero Phosphate Co.* [1878] it was stated that disclosure must be made to an independent Board of Directors who can exercise an independent and intelligent judgement on the transaction.

However, this may be impractical since, in most cases, the promoters would also be the first directors. In such a case, disclosure to the members would be adequate. Disclosures may be made in the memorandum or articles or in a prospectus or offer for sale of shares in the company or in some other way so that "the real truth is disclosed to those who are induced by the promoters to join the company" (*Lagunas Nitrate Co. v Lagunas Syndicate* [1889]).

In *Gluckstein v Barnes* [1900] AC 240, a syndicate purchased a property for £140,000 and resold it to a company formed for the purpose for £180,000. The House of Lords held that the promoters were accountable to the company for the profit made without full disclosure.

Remedies for Breach of Duty of Promoters

A promoter who makes a secret profit out of the promotion of the company, must account for that profit to the company. In the event of non-disclosure of secret profit, the company may rescind the contract made with the promoter or take proceedings for recovery of the secret profit. The contract is voidable at the instance of the company.

To rescind, the company must have done nothing to ratify the contract after finding out about the non-disclosure. See *Gluckstein* v *Barnes* [1900]. Rescission is an equitable remedy and is only possible if the parties can be restored to their original position. The right to rescind is lost if it is not exercised within a reasonable time.

Pre-incorporation Contracts with Outsiders

Under the common law, a contract made on behalf of a company before its incorporation does not bind the company, nor can it be enforced or ratified by the company after incorporation. This is because no legal person, natural or artificial, can enter into a contract before he or it comes into existence and ratification is only possible if the company was in existence when the contract was made.

In *Kelner* v *Baxter* [1866] LR & CP 174 three individuals entered into a contract for the supply of wines and spirits to a proposed hotel which at the time was not yet incorporated as a company. The wines and spirits were delivered and consumed. The company collapsed after incorporation. It was *held* that the three individuals were personally liable on the contract for the wines and spirit.

The above case should be compared with *Newborne* v *Sensolid (Great Britain) Ltd.* [1954] 1 QB 45 where a contract entered into between "Leopold Newborne Ltd. per Leopold Newborne, director" was held to be unenforceable by Mr. Newborne personally when it was later discovered that the company was not incorporated at the time of the making of the contract. The court said that the contract was intended to be with the company and Mr. Newborne could not subsequently substitute himself for the company. The supposed contract was held to be with a non-existing company and therefore there was no contract at all.

See also *Phonogram Ltd.* v *Lane* [1982] where a contract was made by Lane with Phonogram Ltd. "for and on behalf of Fragile Management Limited". The company was never incorporated. It was held that Lane was personally liable for £6,000 which was advanced in respect of Fragile Management Limited. This decision was applied in *Cotronic (UK) Ltd.* v *Dezonie* [1991] BCLC 721[1].

In *Re Northumberland Avenue Hotel Co.* [1886], a promoter entered into a contract for the grant of a building lease prior to the company's incorporation. After incorporation, the company entered into the land and commenced building operations. It was held that the lease was not binding as there was no evidence that a new agreement was entered into after incorporation.

However, in *Howard* v *Patent Ivory Manufacturing Co.* [1888] the owner of property agreed to sell it to a company about to be incorporated. After incorporation, the terms of the agreement were modified. It was held that the modification of the terms created a new agreement entered into by the company and was therefore binding.

In Barbados, the Bahamas and Guyana, statutory provisions now allow a company within a reasonable time after incorporation, to adopt a written contract made on its behalf prior to incorporation.

For example, Section 16 of the Barbados Companies Act provides as follows:

(a) A person who enters into a written contract in the name of or on behalf of a company before it comes into existence is personally bound by the contract and is entitled to the benefits of the contract unless it is expressly stated otherwise in the contract.

(b) Within a reasonable time after a company comes into existence, it may by any action or conduct signifying its intention to be bound thereby adopt a written contract made in its name or on its behalf, before it came into existence.

Promoter's Contract with Company

Where a promoter wishes to sell his own property to the company he must, if he wishes to retain any profits made by the transaction take steps to see that the interests of the company are protected. He must take care that he sells his property to the company through the medium of an independent board of directors or the existing or intended shareholders who can and will exercise an independent judgement on the transaction. In other words, he must make full disclosure to those who had been induced to join the company. If the promoter fails to discharge his obligation, the company may rescind the contract or may sue for breach of his fiduciary duty or compel the promoter to account for the profit. The transaction must be one done while he is a promoter. Promoters may also be liable for untrue or misleading statements in a prospectus. However, the company cannot affirm the contract and also claim for the secret profit made by the promoter.

The modern practice in the case of public companies is that the promoter makes disclosure in a prospectus which has provisions for disclosure.

Remuneration of Promoters

A promoter has no right against the company to payment for his promotion services in the absence of an express contract under seal, since the company cannot make a contract before incorporation and when the contract can be made the consideration given by him will be past.

New Contract

Ratification is not effective with respect to pre-incorporation contracts. However, the company would be bound if a new contract is entered into after incorporation between the company and the other parties – i.e. by novation. A new contract could be inferred from the conduct of the parties after incorporation but the courts would require clear evidence of this. See *Re Northumberland Avenue Hotel Co.* [1886] 33 Ch D 16; *Howard v Patent Ivory Manufacturing Co.* [1888]; *Natal Land and Colonisation Co Ltd.* v *Pauline Colliery and Development Syndicate Ltd.* [1904] AC 120 PC.

Expenses

Lawful expenses incurred by promoters may be paid if permitted by the memorandum or articles of association when the company becomes incorporated. Table A makes provision for the payment of expenses. (See Article 71 p. 65 ante.)

Notes

1. It can be said that the promoters are now personally liable in respect of the pre-incorporation contracts, irrespective of the capacity in which they purport to contract unless there is an agreement to the contrary.

CHAPTER 8

The Rule in Turquand's Case

Internal Management Rule

Under the common law doctrine of constructive notice[1], a person dealing with a company is deemed to know the contents of the company's public documents filed with the Registrar of Companies and their effect with regard to transactions entered into with the company. This was considered to be unfair and burdensome in some respects. As a result, the court responded with the Rule in Turquand's Case which subsequently became known as the "internal management rule".

The Rule in Turquand's case was formulated in the case of *Royal British Bank* v *Turquand* [1855]. The Rule provides that an outsider who deals with a company in reliance of the company's public documents such as the memorandum and articles of association and consistently with those documents, is entitled to assume that all matters of internal management of the company are being complied with. The outsider is entitled to assume that internal proceedings are being properly run and need not enquire into their regularity. Thus if there is an internal procedural irregularity which may affect the validity of a contract with an outsider, the Rule will allow the outsider to ignore the irregularity and to enforce the contract for if the public documents of a company are not being complied with in the internal management of the company, this fact should not prejudice the outsider acting in reliance of the public documents.

The Rule was stated in the Turquand's Case as follows:

"Where there are persons conducting the affairs of a company in a manner which appears to be perfectly consonant with the Articles of Association, then those dealing with them externally are not to be affected by any irregularities in the internal management of the company".

The Turquand's Case involved an action for the return of money borrowed from the bank by the directors of the company. The company's deed of settlement provided that the directors may borrow money if a resolution is passed to permit this in a general meeting. No resolution was passed. It was held that the company was bound, as outsiders were entitled to assume that internal procedures such as the passing of the resolution were complied with. Jervis C.J. said:

". . .the party here, on seeing the deed of settlement, would find out a prohibition from borrowing, but a permission to do so on certain conditions . . . he would have a right to infer the fact of a resolution authorising that which on the face of the document appeared to be legitimately done".

The abolition of constructive notice by the recent legislations of Barbados, the Bahamas and Guyana has superseded the *Turquand's Case* in these territories.

Exceptions to the Rule

The courts have formulated a number of exceptions to the Rule:

1. The Rule does not apply where the person seeking to rely on it knows that matters relating to internal management have not been complied with.
2. The Rule does not apply if the document, which is relied on, is a forgery.
3. The Rule does not apply where a person acting for a company exceeds his authority whether actual or apparent.
4. The Rule does not apply where the transaction is of an unusual nature and the outsider is put on enquiry.
5. The Rule does not apply to an insider who should have knowledge, e.g. a director or secretary of the company for a person is under a duty to inform himself.

6.   The Rule does not apply where the company did nothing to hold out an agent as having authority in the particular transaction.

The Rule is designed to protect outsiders dealing with the company not to protect the company itself. A director, therefore, cannot rely on the Rule.

The recent enactments of Barbados and Guyana have given statutory effect to the Rule. See, for example, section 21(a) of the Barbados Act (1982) where it is provided that a company may not assert against any person who has dealings with the company that any of the articles or by-laws has not been complied with.

Note

1.   See p. 40, supra.

CHAPTER 9

The Raising of Capital

Capital

The word "capital" is commonly used to describe the amount by which the assets of a business exceed its liabilities.

However, in Company Law, the word "capital" is used to mean the "issued share capital" of the company, i.e. the money raised by the issuing of shares by the company, as distinct from "loan capital" which is borrowed money.

There are three main ways for a company to raise its capital:
1. persons taking shares in the company (share capital);
2. persons giving loans to the company (loan capital);
3. retained earnings, i.e. the capitalisation of profits not distributed to shareholders.

Share Capital

The share capital of a company is only one source of funding that a company uses to finance its activities.

In the raising of share capital, a distinction should be made between private companies and public companies.

A public company usually obtains its finance by inviting the public to take shares in the company. However, a public company can only offer its shares to the public subject to certain provisions designed for the protection of those taking up shares. For example, any advertisement of the shares for sale to the public must be accompanied by a "prospectus"[1], and the contents of this document must contain the matters listed in the Schedule to the Companies Act. Prospectuses must be registered with the Registrar on or before publication.

Private companies, on the other hand, are prohibited from selling their shares to the public and there are also restrictions on their rights to transfer shares to non-members as may be specified in the articles of the companies.

Types of Capital

There are many expressions involving the use of the word "capital". Distinction is normally made between the following:

Nominal (or Authorized) Capital

A company limited by shares, or by guarantee and having a share capital, is required to state the amount of its nominal capital in the capital clause of the memorandum of association. This figure shows the maximum number of shares the company is authorized to issue. Shares must not be issued beyond the nominal capital.

Issued Capital

This is that portion of the nominal or authorized capital which has been issued as shares to shareholders. A company is not obliged to issue all its nominal capital at once.

References to "capital" are usually references to *issued* capital. Issued capital cannot exceed the nominal or authorized capital.

Paid-up Capital

This is the amount of issued capital that has been paid up. Shares may be partly paid up or fully paid up.

Uncalled Capital

The difference between the amount paid up and the total value of the issued shares is referred to as the uncalled capital (also unpaid capital).

Uncalled capital is not generally considered to be an asset of the company until it is called up, but a company may mortgage its uncalled capital.

In Barbados and Guyana under their recent legislation, all shares must be fully paid up before they are issued.

Reserve Capital

A company may, by special resolution, resolve that the whole or part of its uncalled capital shall not be called up except in the event of a winding up. This uncalled amount is called the reserve capital. Reserve capital must not be confused with "general reserve" or "reserve fund" which is undistributed profits.

Minimum and Maximum Share Capital

The law in the Region does not prescribe a minimum or maximum share capital for public or private companies. The amount is left to promoters, in the first instance, to fix and later to the directors to determine if any change is required.

Alteration of Share Capital

Companies limited by shares may, in general meeting, if so authorized by its articles, by ordinary resolution, increase its share capital by such amount as is considered expedient.

An increase in share capital is only necessary when all the nominal capital as stated in the memorandum has been issued.

Where there is an increase of share capital beyond that registered, the Registrar must be notified of the increase (normally within *fifteen* days of the increase), which is recorded.

Increase in share capital is normally made with a view of raising further capital for the company or to bring the nominal capital into close relation with the actual assets of the company.

Consolidation and Sub-Division of Shares

The company in general meeting may also consolidate or divide all or any of its share capital into shares of larger or smaller amounts or convert all or any of its paid up shares into stock or vice versa, or cancel shares which at the date of passing of the resolution, have not been taken up, and thus diminish its share capital by the amount of shares cancelled[2].

A consolidation is the merging of a number of shares into one share, e.g. ten "one dollar" shares into one "ten dollar" share.

A sub-division is the reverse of consolidation, e.g. a "ten dollar" share sub-divided into ten "one dollar" shares. A sub-division of shares is not a variation of class rights of other shares not sub-divided even if voting rights have been altered (see *Greenhalgh* v *Arderne Cinemas* [1946]).

Any consolidation, division or conversion must be registered with the Registrar of Companies.

Par Value Shares

With the exception of recent legislation[3], the Region requires companies which have a share capital (unless they are unlimited companies) to divide the total share capital into shares of a fixed amount[4]. Such shares are known as par value shares, i.e. shares that have a nominal value in relation to the total capital.

The proposed share capital, the number of shares into which it is divided, and the nominal value of each share must be stated in the memorandum. The intention is to protect creditors and shareholders. Total par value of company's shares was intended to represent the real value of the company's business. The thinking behind the par value system is that investors in a company would have a method of assessing the worth of the assets of the company and therefore their security for their investment. The system has been criticized as being an unreliable measure of the true worth of the assets of the company as the assets may have appreciated or may have fallen and the actual market price may have no resemblance to the par value.

No par Value Shares

- *CARICOM Recommendation*

A no par value share is one where the price is not attached to a par value, i.e. to a fixed money value, but is determined mainly by market considerations.

The *CARICOM Report* recommended the removal of the par value system in order to prevent deceptions and misunderstandings leaving the prospective investor to estimate the value of a share on the basis of knowledge of the assets of the company regardless of any face value placed on the share.

The Report recommended that all shares created or issued under new legislation should be shares of no par value and that the articles of incorporation for the company should set out the minimum "issued" price in respect of a share or each class of shares if divided into classes.

Barbados and Guyana have adopted the recommendation and have provided that the shares of a company are to be without nominal or par value attached to a share[5]. The result is that a share premium account is now obsolete[6].

Equity Share Capital (equity financing)

Equity share capital consists of those shares that have no prior limitation to the amount a shareholder may receive on a distribution either as a dividend or as a distribution of surplus assets on winding-up of the company. Ordinary shares are, as a rule, the equity share capital of the company. Preference shares are not normally within this category as preference shares usually have a limited right to a fixed dividend and no right to participate in surplus assets in a winding up.

Shares

A share is essentially a unit of account for measuring a member's interest in the company. It is what is referred to as a "chose in action". It has been stated that a share is "the interest of the shareholder in the company measured by a sum of money for the purpose of liability in the first place and of interest in the second but also consisting of a series of mutual commitments entered into by all share holders" – per Farwell J. in *Borland's Trustee* v *Steel* [1901].

Shares are personal property with rights and obligations and can be dealt with as such[7]. But ownership of shares does not constitute part ownership of the assets of the company.

The extent of a shareholder's interest will depend on the kind of shares he holds, as a share gains its values from the rights that are attached to it.

A person who takes shares in a company will become a member of the company. On the other hand, if he lends money to the company, he is not a member but a creditor who will look for security for his loan.

Classes of Shares

Shares may be divided into different classes and the rights of each class may be defined in the memorandum or the articles of association or, in the case of shares created on an increase of capital, by the resolution of the increase.

The Region does not expressly authorize companies to issue shares of different classes, although many of the Acts empower the issue of preference shares if the articles of the company authorize it to do so.

The shares in a company may be all alike, i.e. they all carry the same rights as to voting, dividends and the return of capital in a winding up. But this is not often the case, for a company may have different classes of shares with different rights.

A company may, by virtue of its articles, have power to issue different classes of shares with varying rights. However, any preferential rights given to a class of shares must be clearly defined, as these will be strictly construed against the holder.

To ascertain the rights conferred on a share, reference is to be made to the articles and to the particulars of the terms of issue for the particular class of shares.

In the absence of anything in the articles to the contrary, each share is presumed to be equal in rights and obligations. This presumption can be rebutted by the terms of issue for the shares. Rights may vary considerably. There is an infinite number of combinations.

Classes of shares usually issued are:

(a)   Ordinary shares
(b)   Preference shares
(c)   Deferred shares
(d)   Redeemable shares.

• **Ordinary Shares**

The rights of ordinary shares are the rights that remain after the rights of the other classes of shares are satisfied.

Ordinary shares usually give the shareholder the right to vote, as against the preference shareholder whose voting rights are usually restricted. By this right to vote the ordinary shareholders are given control over the management of the company.

Ordinary shares normally carry the residue of any distributed profits after the preference shares, if any, have received their fixed dividend.

A company may issue non-voting or restricted voting ordinary shares which form a separate class of shares. These shares carry equal rights with ordinary shares except for the voting restriction.

• **Preference Shares**

A company may create a class of shares with certain special rights in order to attract capital. Holders of such shares are said to hold preference shares. There is no precise legal definition of "preference shares". The term is used to denote shares that give their holders certain preferential rights.

The main characteristic of a preference share is usually that it has a preferred fixed dividend, i.e. the dividend payable on it is fixed at a certain figure, e.g. ten percent, and this dividend is payable before the other class of shareholders are paid any dividend. They are designed to appeal to investors who want a steady return on their investment combined with a high level of security. As an investment, they are not attractive in a period of inflation or high interest payment and their importance as a method of financing has declined.

Preference shares can either be cumulative or non-cumulative. They are presumed to be cumulative unless expressly described as non-cumulative. They are cumulative in the sense that if the company cannot pay a dividend in any particular year, it will accumulate from year to year until they are paid. It is non-cumulative in the sense that if a dividend is not paid in any year it will not accumulate for payment in future years. In other words, the preference shareholder will not get a dividend for that year.

It is usual to make it clear that the shares are "cumulative preference shares" when issued.

Preference shares often do not carry voting rights and they do not have priority to a return of capital in a winding up unless the memorandum or articles or terms of issue specifically give them this right. However, it is common for this right to be given, in which case there is no implied right to participate further in the distribution of surplus assets on a winding-up – *Scottish Insurance Corporation* v *Wilsons and Clyde Coal Co.* [1949].

The right to receive the preferred fixed dividend in priority to other classes of shares only exists if a dividend is declared by the company. It is not a right to compel the company to pay the dividend in any event[8].

• Deferred Shares

These are shares that are issued to a promoter or vendor of a business to the company for services rendered or as payment of the business. The right to payment for a dividend is normally deferred until ordinary shareholders have been paid a dividend for the year. These are rarely issued today. Ordinary shares are normally issued instead.

• Redeemable Shares

As a general rule, a company cannot issue redeemable shares since any such redemption is a purchase by the company of its own shares which is a reduction of capital[9].

In recent legislation, the power to redeem preference shares is permitted if a company is authorized to do so by its articles. (See, for example, section 57 and Articles 2-5 of Table A of the First Schedule of the Jamaica Companies Act.)

Redeemable preference shares if permitted are subject to conditions which are designed to safeguard against a reduction of capital.

The *CARICOM Report* has recommended that a public company should have a general power to issue and redeem redeemable shares of any class subject to adequate safeguards against the reduction of capital.

Barbados has adopted this recommendation. See s 41 of the Companies Act, 1982. See also section 4 of the Guyana Companies Act 1991 (not yet in force).

Issue of Shares

The process by which persons take shares in a company is called issuing of shares. It ends with an allotment being made.

The power to issue shares is normally vested in the directors of the company either by the Act, the articles or by the company giving them this power in a general meeting. If the directors are not so authorised they have no power to issue shares. The right to issue shares is subject to any limitation in the Articles of the company.

The power to issue shares cannot be delegated.

The directors' powers to issue shares are governed by fiduciary considerations and must be exercised for the purposes for which it was granted, which is normally to raise funds for the company in order to satisfy its financial needs and to ensure the financial stability of the company.

The issuing of shares by the directors is to be made bona fide for the benefit of the company as a whole. If not so made, it will be presumed to be made to perpetuate the directors' control over the company and would therefore be void (*Percival* v *Wright* [1902]).

Directors are also not entitled to issue shares merely to prevent a take-over offer because they fear that the new controllers will conduct the company in a way which they consider disadvantageous nor simply in order to eliminate the existing majority.

The court will examine the reason for the issue and if the reason was not to raise capital, the issue will be considered an abuse of the directors' powers.

In *Howard Smith Ltd.* v *Ampol Petroleum Ltd.* [1974] 1 ALLER 1126, it was found that the primary purpose of the allotment was to enable the minority shareholders to sell at more advantageous terms by diluting the majority voting power. It was held that directors must not use their fiduciary power over the shares purely for the purpose of destroying the existing majority or creating a new majority. To use their fiduciary power solely for the purpose of shifting the power cannot be related to any purpose for which the power was conferred. The allotment was therefore held to be void.

Ways of becoming a Shareholder

Ways in which a person may become a shareholder in a company with a share capital are :
  (a)   by taking shares in the company by allotment;
  (b)   by taking a transfer of shares from an existing shareholder, either by sale or by gift; or
  (c)   by the operation of law under which the shares of an existing shareholder are devolved or vested in the person, e.g. where the shares of a deceased shareholder devolve on the personal representatives (devolution of shares by operation of law is usually referred to as *transmission* of shares).

Issuing and Allotment of Shares

The process by which members take shares from a company is called issuing the shares and it ends when an allotment is made.

The basic feature of an allotment is that the allottee acquires his shares directly from the company and not from a previous shareholder.

Shares are taken to be allotted when a person acquires the unconditional right to be included in the company's register of members after an application for shares has been made.

In a private company shares cannot be issued to the public. In this case the process is usually informal and is handled by the company secretary or accountant or an attorney-at-law. The articles are to be looked at as to the process.

In a public company shares can be issued to the public but a prospectus must be issued.

Application for Shares

The general law of contract applies to contracts for the allotment of shares in a company. The issuing of a prospectus and application form by a public company is not an offer to take shares in the company in the contractual sense, but merely an invitation to the public to offer or take up shares in the company. It is the applicant for the shares who has completed and submitted the application form to the company who makes the offer for shares in the company and it is the company who accepts or rejects it. The company signifies its acceptance to the applicant by sending him a letter of allotment.

In a rights issue[10] (i.e. an issue of new ordinary shares in proportion to a member's existing holding) the letter of rights sent by the company to holders of existing shares is an offer which on acceptance constitutes a binding contract. If the letter is an "open offer" (i.e. an invitation to shareholders to apply for any number of new shares) the member's reply constitutes the offer.

Conditional Applications

The law of contract requires the acceptance of an offer to be entire. If the acceptance introduces a new term or varies the offer in any way, it will amount in law to a counter-offer which will revoke the original offer and itself would require acceptance by the original offerer. This rule could lead to difficulty where the issue of shares is over-subscribed, i.e. there are more applications for shares than what the company has issued. To avoid the difficulty, the application form is usually worded: "I agree to accept _____ shares or such lesser amount as may be allotted to me". By this, the company is able to accept the applicant's offer by allotting shares less than the number applied for.

Letter of Allotment

An acceptance by the company by letter of allotment must be communicated within a reasonable time.

In *Ramsgate Victoria Hotel Co. Ltd.* v *Montefiore* [1866], M applied for a number of shares in the plaintiff company in June but no allotment was made until November of that year. M refused to accept the shares. It was held that the offer had lapsed as the allotment was not made within a reasonable time.

Pre-emption rights for existing shareholders

Existing shareholders may have a right to be offered shares in proportion to their present holdings whenever a new issue is made. Such rights are normally given by the company's articles[11].

Returns of Allotment

When a company limited by shares makes an allotment, it must (usually within one month) deliver to the Registrar of Companies a return in the prescribed form of the allotments, stating the number and nominal amount of the shares allotted and other required particulars.

Admission to Stock Exchange Listing

Where the shares are to be listed on the Stock Exchange[12], the company must comply with the Stock Exchange rules which set out a number of conditions to be fulfilled including that the company must be a public company and the securities must be freely transferable.

The required contents for listing particulars include:

(a)   details of the company and details of any group of which it is a part;

(b)   details of the shares which are to be issued;

(c)   details of the persons forming the management of the company.

Companies that are listed on the Stock Exchange must comply with continuing obligations to inform the Stock Exchange of incorporation or any major new developments in the sphere of activity of the company which might lead to movements in the price of shares. This is necessary in order to enable holders of the company's securities and the public to assess the performance of the company. Also to be included is the date fixed for any board meeting at which the declaration of a dividend is likely to be made, any proposal to alter the company's capital structure or to buy or sell a major asset.

Prospectus Issues

Where the shares are not to be listed on the Stock Exchange any advertisement of them for sale must be accompanied by a "prospectus".

Any document by which shares are offered to the public is deemed to be a prospectus. The contents of a prospectus are to be found in a Schedule of the Companies Act[13].

A number of remedies are available for negligent or fraudulent mis-statements in a prospectus. The remedies are available against those making the misrepresentations including a promoter or director.

The remedies available are rescission of the contract for the shares and damages for loss suffered. The misrepresentation must have been material and must have induced the person to subscribe for the shares in the company.

In *Smith* v *Chadwick* [1884] the prospectus stated that a certain well known person was a director of the company when in fact the person had withdrawn his consent to be a director before the prospectus was issued. It was held that although the statement in the prospectus was untrue it was not material as the plaintiff had never heard of the person who was named director.

Expert

If a company adopts or relies on or authenticates a report of an expert which is referred to in the prospectus, it will incur liability if the report is false.

In *Re Pacaya Rubber Co.* [1914] a prospectus included a report of an expert on the number and conditions of the rubber trees on the estate. The report was inaccurate. The company was held liable.

Offers

A "direct offer" issue of shares is where the public is invited to subscribe for shares which would be allotted directly by the company.

An "offer for sale" issue is where the whole issue of shares is taken by an "issuing house" which then offers the shares to the public for purchase. This means that the issuing house and not the company has the responsibility for the risk that all the shares may not be sold.

If a company wishes to raise money from existing shareholders, it may seek to do so by way of a "restricted rights offer". This is an offer of more shares to existing shareholders which can only be accepted by them. If the shareholder passes the offer on to others the issue is described as a *rights issue*. In the case of a rights issue the shares are usually offered in a renounceable letter of right. If the shareholder to whom it is addressed does not wish to avail himself of the offer he may renounce his right to do so in favour of another person.

A "public offer" is an invitation to the public at large by a public company to buy shares in the company.

When shares are bought for the first time it is said to be a subscription, the shares are said to be subscribed and the buyer is known as a subscriber.

Another way of disposing of shares is to sell the entire issue to an "issuing house" who will find buyers other than by an offer to the public at large. The company is said to place the shares with their clients and this method is known as the "placing of shares" or *selective marketing*.

Variation of Class Rights

"Variation" means the direct alteration of the rights of a class. (See *Clemens* v *Clemens Brothers Ltd.* [1976].)

The rights attached to any particular class of shares may be varied in accordance with the provisions of the memorandum, the articles or other conditions of issue of shares, but subject to the rights of the minority holders of the class. These rights are usually concerned with voting, dividends and distribution of the assets on a winding up of the company.

It is usual for the articles to provide that members who own a certain class of shares, who did not consent to or vote in favour of the variation, to apply to the Court within twenty-one days of the variation for cancellation of the variation.

If, however, the class rights are mentioned in the memorandum or the articles but they are silent as to variation, then variation requires the agreement of all the members of the company or the sanction of the Court.

If the class rights are stated in the articles or terms of issue then the variation requires the written consent of holders of three-quarters of the shares of that class or the passing of an extraordinary resolution at a class meeting.

The Courts are reluctant to describe most changes of class rights as a variation. There is no variation in the following situations:

1. The issue of new shares which rank equally with existing shares does not vary the class rights of the existing shares. See *White* v *Bristol Aeroplane Co. Ltd.* [1953] where the company issued new preference shares and ordinary shares thereby decreasing the effectiveness of the voting rights in the existing shares.

   In practice, this is the most common and important way in which rights are changed since the new issue reduces or dilutes a person's share in the wealth of the company and affects his voting rights.

2. Class rights are not varied by subdivision of other shares which has the effect of increasing the voting rights of those shares – *Greenhalgh* v *Arderne Cinemas Ltd.* [1946] where 50 preference shares of one class were sub-divided into 10 preference shares.

3. The cancellation of shares where those were entitled to priority in the repayment of capital in a winding up – *House of Fraser* v *ACGE Investments Ltd.* [1987].

4. A bonus issue to ordinary shareholders which deprives preference shareholders of their rights to participate in surplus assets on a winding up is not a variation of the preference shareholder's rights – *Dimbula Valley (Ceylon) Tea Co. Ltd.* v *Laurie* [1961] Ch 353.

In all these cases, the class rights involved remained the same – to have one vote per share or to participate in surplus assets – even though the shares, as a result of the change, were less valuable to the holders.

Share Certificates

A member's share certificate certifies that he is the registered holder of a specified number of shares of a certain class.

Under the Acts of the Region, a certificate under the common seal of the company specifying the shares held by a member is *prima facie* evidence of the title of the member to the shares mentioned in the certificate.

A share certificate gives rise to estoppel, both as to title and the amount paid on the shares, as against the company and in favour of a person who has relied on the certificate. If a person suffers loss because of an untrue statement on the share certificate, the company must compensate him – *Re Bahia and San Francisco Railway Co. Ltd.* [1868].

It is usually provided that a share certificate is to be made out by the company and delivered to the member within two months from the date when a transfer was lodged for registration or three months after allotment.

Transfer of Shares

Shares are capable of being transferred as personal property in the manner provided in the articles subject to a proper instrument of transfer[14] having been completed and delivered to the company.

Every shareholder has a right to transfer his shares when he likes unless the articles provide otherwise. The articles may impose fetters upon the right of transfer.

In the case of a private company, the articles usually restrict the right to transfer shares. There is normally a pre-emption clause which restricts transfer to a non-member so long as a member can be found to purchase the shares at a fair price to be determined in accordance with the articles.

The articles may also provide that the directors have the power to refuse registration of a transfer without giving reasons. The court will not interfere with the directors' exercise of such a power, unless it is proved that they were not acting bona fide in the interest of the company. (See *Tett* v *Phoenix Property & Investment Co. Ltd.* [1986] BCLC 599.)

Procedure for the Transfer of a Share

Entry in the register of members is the decisive step by which a person becomes the legal owner of shares.

To obtain the legal ownership of shares:

(a)   a proper instrument of transfer[15] is delivered to the company;

(b) stamp duty on the instrument is to be paid;

(c) share certificate must be sent to the company.

The procedure to be followed will depend on whether the member is transferring all his shares or only a part of it.

The basic transfer procedure, in the case of transfer of all the shares on a share certificate, is that the registered holder completes and signs the standard form of transfer and delivers it with his share certificate to the transferee who completes the transfer and has it stamped with stamp duty before delivering it with the share certificate to the company for registration. The company issues to the transferee a new certificate and cancels the old one. The transferee's name is then entered in the register of members.

If the shareholder is only transferring a part of his shares as represented by the share certificate, the procedure is somewhat different as he will not want to part with his share certificate to the transferee. In such a case, the holder sends his signed instrument of transfer with his share certificate to the company. The company will retain the share certificate and return the instrument of transfer endorsed "certificate lodged" with company. The shareholder then delivers the instrument of transfer to the transferee who completes it and get it stamped. He then sends the instrument of transfer to the company. The company then cancels the old certificate and issues two new certificates – one showing the transferor's shares and the other the transferee's shares. Their names are then entered in the register of members.

If the company does not refuse to register a transfer then it must, within two months of the transfer being lodged for registration, have ready for delivery a new certificate.

If the signature of a shareholder is forged on an instrument of transfer then the instrument is void and the original holder still holds the shares. However, a person who parts with money on the faith of a certificate issued by the company as a result of a forged transfer in the belief that he is buying shares, is entitled to rely on the certificate and the company is liable to compensate him for his loss – *Re Bahia and San Francisco Railway Co. Ltd.* [1868].

SPECIMEN FORM

INSTRUMENT OF TRANSFER OF SHARES

COMPANY

TRANSFEROR:

Name:
Address:
Occupation:

TRANSFEREE

Name:
Address:
Occupation:

NUMBER OF SHARES

CONSIDERATION

DATE

SIGNED BY THE TRANSFEROR : _____

In the presence of:

SIGNED BY THE TRANSFEREE : _____

In the presence of:

Notes

1. See pp. 92–93 infra.
2. Such cancellation is not considered to be a reduction of share capital.
3. That is, those of Barbados and Guyana but not the Bahamas - see pp. 7-8, supra.
4. See share capital clause in the Memorandum of Association, p. 42, supra.
5. See, e.g, s 26 (2) of the Barbados Companies Act.
6. See p. 105, infra.
7. A person may transfer his shares to someone else either by sale or gift; but this is subject to the company's articles.
8. See chapter 13, pp. 116 - 120, infra.
9. See chapter 10, pp. 100 - 106, infra.
10. In a "rights issue", the existing shareholders are given "pre-emption rights" (rights of first refusal).
11. See, "rights issue", p. 94, infra.
12. Stock Exchanges are in Barbados, Jamaica and Trinidad and Tobago.
13. See, for example, the Third Schedule to the Companies Act of Jamaica.
14. See p. 98, infra for a specimen instrument of transfer. See also Article 19 of Table A, p. 57, supra.
15. See p. 98, infra.

CHAPTER 10

Maintenance of Capital

Need to Maintain Capital

The common law has developed a number of rules designed to ensure that a company's share capital remains intact as a fund to which creditors of the company could look to as a security for their debts. A reduction of capital is generally illegal unless authorized by legislation – *Trevor* v *Whitworth* [1887] 12 App Cas 409.

The common law rules relating to the maintenance of capital were designed to ensure:

1. that the money or other consideration that the company receives from shareholders for their shares is equal to the nominal value and any premium payable for the shares;

2. that the money received by the company is maintained as a capital fund to which creditors of the company can look to as security for their debts.

In practice, the money received from shareholders is used to purchase the company's corporate assets, i.e. the land, buildings, plant and stock, and creditors take charges over these assets.

The rules relating to the maintenance of capital do not prevent companies from obtaining loan capital or incurring debts that exceed the amount of share capital raised.

The Fundamental Rule

It is a fundamental principle of company law that share capital must be maintained by the company and that the company should not use the money from share capital except for the purposes as set out in the objects clause in the memorandum of association i.e. it must be used to carry out the business of the company for which it was formed.

The principle that share capital must be maintained means that:
1. Paid up share capital must not be returned to the members;
2. Members' liability in respect of the share capital not yet paid up must not be reduced;
3. Shares must be fully paid for.

Because of this principle, the rules developed by the courts prevent a company from purchasing its own shares, or issuing shares at a discount or paying dividends out of capital.

Matters to be Considered

The maintenance of share capital involves consideration of the following matters:
(a) the consideration paid for shares issued
(b) company purchasing its own shares
(c) financial assistance by the company for purchase of its shares
(d) reduction of capital
(e) issuing of shares at a discount
(f) redeemable shares
(g) payment of dividends
(h) issuing of shares at a premium.

• The Consideration paid for Shares Issued

The basic common law rule states that as long as the company received some consideration for the shares, it was immaterial whether they were issued for cash. The consideration may be in the form of property, goods or services (i.e. consideration may be other than for cash). In other words, shares may be paid for in money or money's worth (including goodwill and know-how). The court is generally very reluctant to decide the value of non-cash assets and will normally accept the valuation given unless there is fraud or dishonesty (*Re Wagg Ltd.* [1897]).

However, shares must always be paid for. Until paid, it is a debt owed to the company.

- **Purchase by a Company of its own Shares**

It is a basic principle of the common law that a company may not purchase its own shares – *Trevor* v *Whitworth* [1887]. To allow a company to purchase its own shares would, in effect, be to return share capital back to the shareholders. Acquisition of its shares by a company, therefore, is a reduction of capital. In recent years, this prohibition has been relaxed for the benefit of the company and the shareholders, provided the position of creditors and other interested parties can be protected and it is authorized by the articles.

- **Financial Assistance for the Purchase of the Company's own Shares**

Instead of a company buying its own shares, it could provide financing for a person to buy its own shares. This however, is tantamount to a company buying its own shares. In *Selangor United Rubber Estates Ltd* v *Cradock* (No 3)[1968] 1 WLR 1555, for example, it was held that a company cannot provide funds for the purchase of its own shares.

This prohibition may be relaxed for private companies but subject to a number of procedural restrictions, e.g. it must be by special resolution; there is no reduction of the company's net assets; or it is made out of distributable profits and supported by a statutory declaration to that effect.

Financial assistance includes the giving of gifts, loans, guarantees, securities and other financial assistance that reduces the company's net assets to a material extent.

Modern legislation[1] generally provides for financial assistance to be given by a company in the following circumstances:

(i)   the company may lend money where its ordinary business is the lending of money;

(ii) it may provide money in accordance with an employee share scheme for the acquisition of fully paid shares in the company or its holding company;

(iii) it may make loans to employees, other than directors, to enable them to acquire fully paid shares in the company or its holding company.

• Reduction of Share Capital

A reduction of capital is generally illegal unless authorized by statute. Generally, legislation provides that a company can only reduce its share capital (i.e. the authorized share capital) with the approval of the court and any intended alteration must be authorized by the articles and must be carried out on the authority of a special resolution[2].

Before any reduction of capital is made, consideration must be given to any effect the reduction may have on existing voting rights of members.

If a reduction in capital affects creditors, the court will not confirm the reduction unless the creditors agree, or are paid off, or are given security.

In addition to the interests of the creditors, the court will ensure that the reduction in the share capital is equitable between the various classes of shareholders – *Re Holders Investment Trust Ltd.* [1971].

In *Carruth* v *Imperial Chemical Industries* [1937] a company's capital consisted of ordinary shares and deferred shares. The company reduced the value of the deferred shares and converted every four deferred shares into one ordinary share. The company's articles permitted a reduction of capital as may seem expedient. As the reduction strengthened the company's financial base, it was upheld by the court.

If a reduction involves a reduction of liability in respect of uncalled capital or a return of capital, a list of creditors entitled to object to the reduction must be settled and consent of the creditors must be obtained.

The court will generally sanction a reduction in share capital, unless the reduction is unfair to the creditors, the shareholders, and the public, who may have dealings with the company. The primary concern of the court is to be assured that the interests of the existing creditors are protected, but the question of whether there should be reduction is a domestic matter for the company to decide. However, the court must be satisfied that the cause of the reduction was properly put to the members so that they could make an informed decision.

If the court approves a reduction, it makes an order confirming the reduction. The order confirming the reduction is to be delivered to the Registrar of Companies together with a minute stating the company's new capital structure. The Registrar will then issue a certificate specifying the new share capital of the company.

Certain types of reduction, which will not affect creditors are generally permitted if the articles so provide, usually by ordinary resolution of a general meeting, without the need for court confirmation, e.g. the cancellation of un-issued shares is so permissible.

It is to be remembered that any reduction of share capital would entail an alteration of the memorandum of the company which can only be done by special resolution as provided under the Companies Acts.

• Shares Issued at a Discount

The general rule is that shares must not be issued at a discount, i.e. they must not be issued as fully paid for a consideration which is less than the nominal or par value.

If shares are allotted at a discount, the allottee is liable to pay the company the full nominal value of the share and any subsequent purchaser who is aware that the shares were issued at a discount is also liable. See, *Ooregum Gold Mining Co. of India Ltd.* v *Roper* [1892] A.C. 125.

• Redeemable Shares

Payments made by a company to redeem shares may constitute a reduction of capital, if those payments are made out of capital, since the company will be purchasing its own shares.

Redeemable shares are issued shares which, at the option of the company or the shareholder, can be repurchased by the company. Such a repurchase must be funded from the proceeds of a new issue of shares or from distributable profits, and in the latter case a sum equivalent to the repaid capital must be transferred to a capital account called the capital redemption reserve, which can be used to finance an issue of bonus shares allocated to existing shareholders.

Normally, therefore, shares are not redeemable, except with the consent of the court, as this is a reduction of capital.

The Acts in the Region, however, permit a company to issue redeemable shares, if the articles allow it to make the issue. The redeemable shares may be redeemed only out of distributable profits, revenue reserves or out of the proceeds of a fresh issue of shares made for this purpose.

The shares redeemed must be treated as cancelled on redemption and the company's issued share capital is to be diminished by the amount of their nominal value. The authorized share capital is not affected by the redemption.

If the shares are redeemed out of distributable profits, a capital reserve must be formed in order to keep the total share capital constant.

Usually notice of any redemption must be given to the Registrar within one month.

• Issue of Shares at a Premium

It is usual to issue shares at a price above their nominal or par value, i.e. at a premium.

When shares are issued at a premium, the premium is to be put into a share premium account which can only be used for the following purposes:

(a)   to finance an issue of fully paid bonus shares to members;
(b)   to write off preliminary expenses;
(c)   to write off commissions paid, or discounts allowed or the expenses of an issue of shares or debentures;
(d)   to provide the premium payable on the redemption of any debentures of the company;
(e)   where redeemable shares are issued at a premium, to provide the premium payable on redemption.

Share premiums are treated as capital. They cannot be distributed as dividends. In doing so, it is recognized that what is important is the actual value received for the shares when issued and not the nominal value.

CARICOM Report

The *CARICOM Report* recommends that a company should be able to reduce its share capital subject to certain safeguards relating to its solvency. It recommends that the general circumstances in which the company may reduce capital should be prescribed but that there should be no requirement for application to, and confirmation of, the court.

Barbados and Guyana have given effect to this recommendation.

Notes

1. See, for example, the proviso to section 54 of the Companies Act of Jamaica.
2. See Table A, Article 44 (d); see p. 62, supra.

CHAPTER 11

Loan Capital

Borrowing is an important method of financing the activities of a company. Loan capital is used to refer to sums borrowed by the company other than by short or medium term borrowings. It may comprise indebtedness of the company secured by a debenture[1], by a mortgage or other securities. Holders of loan capital are not, as such, members of the company.

As an alternative to obtaining funds by an issue of shares, a company may, if authorized, either expressly or by implication, borrow money. Loans to a company are usually evidenced by a document called a debenture. As with any loan, the lender will usually require some security or charge to secure his investment against which he can have a right of recourse if the loan is not repaid in time.

Power to Borrow

A trading company has an implied power to borrow and to give security for loans made to it. A non-trading company must be expressly empowered to borrow.

In any event, the power to borrow is usually given expressly in the objects clause in the memorandum. Limits may, however, be imposed upon the total amount which can be borrowed, or more usually, upon the amounts which directors can raise without going to a general meeting. If no limits are imposed, the power to borrow is unlimited. It is usually provided in the articles that the directors cannot borrow in excess of the nominal share capital without approval of the company in general meeting.

A private company may borrow as soon as it is incorporated. A public company must first obtain a certificate of compliance with the capital requirements of the public company and the Registrar must issue a certificate to commence business.

The power to borrow includes the power to charge the assets of the company by way of security to the lender. Borrowing in excess of the limit imposed in the objects clause or borrowing for a purpose which is ultra vires, is *void*.

The power to borrow is normally exercised by the directors. A member may bring proceedings to restrain borrowing which is ultra vires the company.

The security (including debentures) given by a company for a loan will often constitute a charge on the assets of the company. The charge may be a fixed charge or a floating charge[2].

Debentures

A debenture has been defined as a document which either creates a debt or acknowledges it and any document which fulfills either of these conditions is a debenture. (*Levy* v *Abercorris Slate and Slab Co.* [1887] Ch D. 260.)

The debenture is a document issued by a company acknowledging its indebtedness under a loan and setting out its terms. The expression is usually used to describe the loan itself.

A debenture need not be, but is usually made under a seal.

A debenture usually creates a fixed or floating charge on the company's assets as security for the loan, although a debenture may be unsecured, i.e. no charge is created on the assets of the company.

A debenture may be a single debenture, evidencing a large sum of money lent to the company by a single debenture holder, or the company can create a loan fund known as "debenture stock" which is issued to a number of debenture holders, each of whom is given a debenture stock certificate evidencing a proportion of the total loan he is entitled to.

A debenture may or may not be one of a series ranking *pari passu*, i.e. each lender has an equal right to repayment.

A debenture is always for a specified sum, e.g. $100, which can be transferred in its entirety. It is usually redeemable at a fixed future date. The power to issue debentures is usually set out in the company's objects clause in the memorandum.

A legal mortgage or guarantee may be a form of debenture.

Trust Deeds

When a series of debentures are used by a number of debenture holders, a trust deed is normally drawn up. Under the deed, the assets of the company are charged to trustees who can act promptly to protect the interests of all the debenture holders in case of default by the company. Under the deed, the company undertakes to pay the debenture holders their principal and interest.

The deed usually empowers the trustees to appoint a receiver to protect the property charged if the company defaults in payment of the principal and interest. The receiver will be empowered to sell the assets which are the subject to the charge. Trustees, though appointed to protect debenture holders, are normally paid by the company under the terms of the debentures.

Charges

Debentures normally give to the holders a charge over the company's assets. A charge over the assets of a company gives a creditor a prior claim to payment of his debt out of the assets charged over other creditors of the company.

Charges are of two kinds:

1. Fixed or Specific Charge – this is a charge on a particular or definite piece of property, e.g. charge on the land, plant and machinery of the company (often called a mortgage);

    A fixed charge attaches to the assets charged as soon as the charge is created, and the chargee has an immediate proprietory interest in the assets charged. It is similar to an ordinary mortgage and restrictions are imposed on the company, so that it cannot deal with the assets charged without the consent of the debenture holders or their trustees.

A company usually remains in possession but cannot sell or dispose of the assets which are subject to a fixed charge without the consent of the holders of the charge.

2. Floating Charge – this is a charge on all the assets or on a class of assets of the company, present and future, i.e. assets from time to time including fixed assets and circulating assets (stock). A floating charge does not give the chargee any proprietary interest in the assets charged at the time of creation. Rather it "floats" until it "crystallizes". Until it crystallizes, the company can deal freely with the assets charged. When it crystallizes the "floating" charge becomes a "fixed" charge.

In *Re Yorkshire Woolcombers Association Ltd.* [1903] Ch 284, Romer LJ identified three characteristics of a floating charge:

1 it is a charge on a class of assets both present and future

1 the class of assets is changing in the ordinary course of business

1 until the charge crystallizes, the company can carry on business in the ordinary way with regard to that class of assets. (It can even give fixed charges over the particular assets which are subject to the floating charge unless this is expressly prohibited.)

The last characteristic is what makes floating charges attractive, in that a company can raise money on stock, book debts and other assets that are constantly changing and can still carry on the business as usual, until there is a default and the charge crystallizes. (See *Siebe Gorman & Co. Ltd.* v *Barclays Bank Ltd.* [1979].)

A floating charge becomes a fixed charge (i.e. it is said to crystallize), when an event happens which allows the debenture holders (or their trustees) to take possession of the assets or appoint a receiver[3].

Events crystallizing a floating charge into a fixed charge will be stipulated in the debenture or trust deed.

Events that usually cause a crystallization are:

(a)   the liquidation of the company;

(b)   the cessation of the company's business;

(c)   the active intervention of the debenture holders, generally by way of an appointment of a receiver, in order to take steps to enforce the security.

• Registration of Charges

In some of the regional territories, certain charges created by a company are required to be registered in two places:

1.   in a register of charges to be kept by the company at its registered office;

2.   with the Registrar of Companies (which must be done within the prescribed time, usually within twenty-one days of the date of creation, unless the time is extended on an application to the courts).

A copy of the instrument creating the charge is to be kept at the registered office and be available for inspection by members of the public.

If a registrable charge is not registered with the Registrar of Companies, it becomes void against other creditors of the company and against the liquidator. It is not void against the parties themselves, i.e. between the company and the chargee or creditor.

The loan secured by a void charge becomes payable immediately.

It is to be remembered that a debenture holder is a creditor of the company and, as such, has the remedies of a creditor, e.g. it can sue the company for the debt or it can petition the court for a winding up order.

The holder of a subsequent charge which was duly registered may claim priority over an earlier charge which was not registered.

• Extension of Time for Registration

Provisions are normally made to make it possible to apply to the Court for an order to extend the time for registration, if non-registration was accidental or for some other sufficient cause or it is just and equitable for the time to be extended. Application may be made by the company or any interested person.

Registration of charges creates certainty for those lending to the company, in that they can identify from the public register which is maintained by the Registrar of Companies, which assets are already subject to a charge.

The aim of disclosure through registration is to inform creditors of the amount of assets of the company that are charged or are available as security for a loan.

Chargees themselves can deliver particulars of the charge to the Registrar.

The following charges are registrable in the register of charges kept by the Registrar:

(a)   a charge to secure debentures
(b)   a floating charge
(c)   a charge on uncalled share capital
(d)   a charge on land
(e)   a charge on book debts
(f)   a charge on goodwill, patents, trademarks and copyrights
(g)   a charge created by a bill of sale
(h)   a charge on calls made but not paid.

The Registrar is required to keep a Register of Charges in respect of all the charges against a company.

Notes

1.   It is only a public company which may invite the public to take up debentures.
2.   See pp. 109-110, supra.
3.   See chapter 12, p. 113, infra.

CHAPTER 12

Receivers and Managers

Receiver and Manager

A receiver is an individual appointed to take control of another person's property. We have seen that a debenture may provide for the appointment of a receiver by the debenture holder in the event of a breach by the borrower/company of one of the conditions of the debenture[1].

The function of a receiver when appointed by a debenture holder is to get in and sell the assets charged and repay the debenture holders, but subject to the rights of prior secured creditors. The appointment of a receiver will depend upon the terms of the debenture (or trust deed) and the nature of the charge.

The purpose of appointing a receiver is to protect the rights of the debenture holders to the assets of the company which are the subject of the charge.

Notice of appointment must be given to the Registrar of Companies (usually within seven days of the appointment)[2]. An entry is also to be made in the register of charges kept by the company.

If it is desired that the business of the company should be carried on, then a manager should be appointed. The receiver himself may be appointed "receiver and manager". It will be difficult for a "manager" to be appointed unless the debenture covers a floating charge over the assets of the company.

A receiver may be appointed by the Court to collect and protect property. If appointed by the Court, the receiver is an officer of the Court. He is not an agent of the debenture holders or the company. He must receive court sanction in order to carry on the business of the company. An application to the Court is usually made if the debenture does not provide for the appointment of a receiver and the security is in jeopardy.

The fact that a receiver or a receiver and manager is appointed must be shown on every invoice, order and business letter of the company.

When a receiver is appointed, he supersedes the company in the conduct of the business and has the sole authority to deal with the charged property. The company's power to deal with its assets is therefore suspended. The director's powers are also suspended. Nevertheless, the directors still remain in office and are liable for any defaults of the company, for example, to submit annual returns to the Registrar of Companies. The directors can exercise such of their powers as have not been passed to the receiver, e.g. they may convene a general meeting to pass a resolution to wind up the company. They may also sue on behalf of the company if the receiver does not wish to pursue such an action – *Newhart Developments Ltd.* v *Co-operative Commercial Bank Ltd.* [1978] QB 814.

Directors of a company in receivership may cause the company to sue the receiver for breach of duty.

A receiver when appointed, will enter into possession, carry on the business (if appointed manager), collect the assets and, if necessary, sell all or any of those assets to pay off the amount owing on the debenture.

Out of the proceeds he will pay the expenses of the company in accordance with the priority rules, he will pay himself and then pay the debenture holders what is due to them by way of principal and interest.

A receiver is personally liable on the contracts entered into by him but he is entitled to be indemnified out of the company's assets in priority to the debenture holders.

A receiver who is also appointed as a manager is under a duty to preserve the goodwill as well as the assets of the company. He must obtain the Court's approval to borrow money.

If the receiver is appointed by the Court or by the debenture holders as their agents, his appointment dismisses the employees of the company. An appointment under the debenture, however, is normally as agent of the company, in which case the appointment does not terminate contracts of employment with the company. (See *Reid* v *Explosives Co Ltd.* [1887]; and *Griffiths* v *S of S for Social Services* [1974].)

The receiver may apply to the Court for directions in relation to any connected with the performance of his duties.

When the receiver ceases to act, he will:

(a) prepare an abstract of receipts and expenses;

(b) give notice to the Registrar of Companies;

(c) surrender possession back to the company.

The main distinction between a receiver and a liquidator is that the receiver merely represents the debenture holders who have appointed him with control of the assets which are their security. His task is to obtain payment of which is owed to them. On the other hand, a liquidator is appointed to wind-up a company, i.e. to realize all the assets of the company, pay all the debts and distribute any surplus to the shareholders. At the end of a liquidation the company is dissolved — which need not be so when a receiver is appointed.

The receiver has a duty to exercise his powers honestly and in good faith. This duty is owed to the company and to persons who have charges over the company's property. He must take reasonable care to obtain the true market value of the property which is the subject of the charge - *Downsview Nominees Ltd* v *First City Corporation Ltd.* [1993] AC 295 PC.

(For statutory provisions as to the duties of a receiver, see section 283 of the Barbados Companies Act and for general provisions, see sections 275 - 287. See also sections 324-332 of the Comapnies Act of Jamaica.)

Notes

1.   See p. 108, supra.
2.   Immediately in the case of Barbados: see s 283 of the Barbados Act.

CHAPTER 13

Dividends

Payment of Dividends

Commercial companies are usually formed with the main object of earning profits for their shareholders. Profits are usually distributed in the form of dividends.

Dividends are payments made to shareholders out of the profits of the company. Dividends are only to be paid out of profits. The payment of dividends are to be found in the company's articles but no express power is necessary for the company to pay out dividends. The articles usually provide that dividends are to be declared by the company in a general meeting and that no dividend should exceed the amount recommended by the directors (see Table A - Articles 95-102 at p. 69, supra).

The payment of a dividend should be distinguished from the payment of interest. The payment of interest is usually on a loan obtained from creditors and is a debt owed by the company. It can be paid out of assets.

Shareholders do not have an automatic right to the payment of a dividend even if the company has made huge profits. Dividends are only payable when they are declared and a dividend is not a debt owing by the company to a shareholder until it is declared.

Dividends are distributed amongst the members in proportion to their shareholdings and in accordance with their rights as shareholders. The articles normally provide that dividends are to be paid according to the amounts paid upon the shares (see Table A - Article 98 at p. 69, supra).

Preference shareholders usually have a fixed rate of dividend[1]. Dividends to ordinary shareholders will vary from year to year depending on the profits made and the rate declared.

In practice, the directors determine what dividends are to be paid. The directors are not obliged to recommend the distribution of the whole of the profits made. Instead, they may place all or part of it in reserves as they may consider that it is more prudent to retain the profits within the company for use of the company than to recommend payment of a dividend.

A shareholder has no right to a dividend before it is declared. This applies to preference shareholders as well as ordinary shareholders.

Instead of paying a dividend, a company may apply its profits in paying up unissued shares which is issued to members as fully paid bonus shares.

In the case of private companies it may be preferable, for tax purposes, to distribute the profits as directors' fees and salaries instead of dividends.

If the directors do not recommend the payment of a dividend, the members cannot overrule their decision by passing a resolution at a general meeting declaring that a dividend be paid – *Scott v Scott* [1943].

The articles may provide for the payment of an interim dividend by the directors. If this is so, the directors may declare an interim dividend during the financial year. However, if it is not paid it is not a debt owed by the company.

In the absence of anything to the contrary in the articles, a company cannot be compelled to declare a dividend and no action can be brought if no dividend has been declared.

Before recommending the payment of a dividend the directors should have a complete and detailed list of the company's assets and liabilities to see what profits have been made. They should not rely for their value merely on the auditors – *Re City Equitable Fire Insurance Co. Ltd.* [1925].

Assets Available for Dividend

No dividend may be paid out of capital, as this would operate as reduction of capital and therefore illegal – *Trevor v Withworth* [1887].

Loans or depreciation of circulating capital incurred during a year must be made good before paying a dividend for that year but loss or depreciation of fixed capital may be ignored.

In *Lee v Neuchatel Asphalte Co.* [1889], Lindley CJ said:

> "There is nothing at all in the Acts about how dividends are to be paid, nor how profits are to be reckoned; all that is left, and very judiciously and properly left, to the commercial world. It is not subject for an Act of Parliament to say how accounts are to be kept; what is to be put into a capital account, what into an income account, is left to men of business".

In that case a company was formed to acquire and work a concession from the Neuchatel Government for quarrying bituminous rocks and mineral products. The concession was due to expire in 1907. In 1887 there was a profit shown on revenue account and the company proposed to pay a dividend. A shareholder objected on the grounds that:

(1) a large part of the capital had been lost;
(2) the assets were not equal to the share capital; and
(3) the concession being a wasting asset, dividing its annual proceeds was dividing the capital assets of the company.

The court held on none of these grounds could the company be restrained from declaring a dividend.

In *Verner v General and Commercial Investment Trust* [1894] 2 Ch 239 (CA) the business of a company was to invest its funds in shares and other securities, its income being derived from the dividends on the shares it held. Owing to a fall in the market values of its investments, the assets of the company were greatly depreciated in value, but the income for the year exceeded the expenses. An action was brought on behalf of the debenture holders to restrain the company from declaring a dividend without first providing for the loss of capital. Held, the loss was a loss of fixed capital and need not be made good before a dividend was declared. Lindley L.J. said:

> "fixed capital may be sunk and lost, and yet ... the excess of current receipts over current payments may be divided, but ... floating or circulating capital must be kept up, as otherwise it will enter into and form part of such excess, in which case to divide such excess without deducting the capital which forms part of it will be contrary to law".

Effect of Paying Dividends out of Capital

All directors who are knowingly parties to the payment of dividends out of capital, e.g. where bad debts are knowingly entered as assets, are jointly and severally liable to the company to replace the amount of dividends so paid, with interest, and ratification is impossible so as to bind the company. In such a case they are entitled to be indemnified by each shareholder who received dividends, knowing them to be paid out of capital, to the extent of the dividends received.

The principle that a company's capital must be maintained requires that dividends are only to be paid out of accumulated realized profits so far as these are not already distributed or capitalized. "Accumulated realized profits" are profits reduced to cash in hand.

It is not clear however as to what is "realized profits", and the Courts will be guided by modern accounting practice.

"Profits" imply a comparison between the state of a business at two specific dates usually separated by an interval of a year. The fundamental meaning is the amount gained by the business during that year.

Undistributed profits of past years may be brought forward into the current year and distributed in the form of dividends.

When an asset is revalued and a profit recognized, it is not clear whether the profit can be distributed to shareholders as dividends.

In *Dimbula Valley (Ceylon) Tea Co.* v *Laurie* [1961], the Privy Council held that it was permissible to make a distribution on the strength of an unrealized accretion of fixed assets.

Capitalization of Profits

Capitalization of profits can come about by the issuing to members of bonus shares credited as fully paid. Capitalization must be provided for in the articles and the nominal share capital must be sufficient for the issuing of bonus shares.

When profits are capitalized, the profits available for dividend are retained by the company. Instead of paying a dividend the unissued shares are issued as fully paid bonus shares and are allotted to shareholders in proportion to their shareholdings. In such a case, there is said to be a "bonus issue".

(For Capitalization of Profits see Table A, Article 128 of the Jamaica Companies Act).

Creation of Reserve Fund

The general practice of companies is not to distribute as dividends the total profits but to carry forward a part to create a reserve fund to make provision for meeting its liabilities later on.

A reserve fund may at any time be distributed as dividend or employed in any other way as authorized by the articles.

Principles to Apply

(1) A company can usually pay dividends out of its revenue profits, without first making good a loss, realized or unrealized, of fixed capital, although this might be commercially unwise in the case of a realized loss.

(2) Although a loss of fixed capital need not be made good before a dividend is declared out of profits, a loss of circulating capital during the year must first be made good.

(3) A company can pay dividends out of the profits of any one year, without first making good the losses of previous years. Thus a company, which has operated at a loss and thus accumulated a deficit on revenue account, may distribute revenue profits of subsequent years without either making good any part of the accrued loss or canceling the loss by reducing its capital.

(4) A dividend may be declared out of profits in a reserve fund, i.e. undistributed profits from previous years, which profits have not been capitalized.

(5) Unless restrained by its articles, a company can pay dividends out of a realized profit on the sale of fixed assets, provided that upon a balance of account there has been an accretion to paid-up capital.

Note

1.   See p. 87, supra.

CHAPTER 14

Membership

The members of a company are:
- (a) the subscribers of the memorandum of association who become members on incorporation; and
- (b) every other person who agrees to become a member and whose name is entered on the register of members. This can be by allotment, by transfer or by transmission of shares.

The subscribers of a memorandum of association are the first members of the company as from the date of incorporation. They are deemed to have agreed to become members of the company. On registration of the company, their names are to be entered in the register of members, but neither this entry nor any allotment of shares is a condition precedent for membership.

Subject to the above, entry on the register of members is necessary to constitute membership. Mere delivery of an instrument of transfer of shares to the company does not make the transference a member. However, the fact that a person's name has been entered in the register is not itself sufficient to make that person a member. The person must have agreed to become a member.

Register of Members

A company must keep and maintain a register of its members[1] showing their names and addresses, the number of shares which each one holds, the class of shares, the numbers given for the shares, the amount paid up and the dates when each member became and ceased to be a member.

The register must be kept at the company's registered office or some other office of the company if the maintenance of a register is done there. Anyone may inspect the register of members during office hours.

If a share is held jointly by two or more persons, then each person is a member of the company.

In addition to agreeing to become a member, the shareholder's name must appear on the register of members for him to have that status. If his name has not yet been entered, he may be a beneficial owner of the shares concerned but he is not entitled to the full rights of membership.

A company's register of members is prima facie evidence of the matters recorded therein.

The company may close the register of members for not more than thirty days in each year, giving notice by advertisement in a newspaper which is circulated in the district of its registered office. The closure should be authorized by a resolution of the directors.

The company cannot enter in the register, a statement that it has a lien on the shares of a member and cannot insist on putting on the register anything except what is required by statute to be inserted in it.

Rectification of Register

The directors of a company may rectify the register of members if there is no dispute and the circumstances are such that a court would order rectification; but ordinarily an order of the court should be obtained to remove a name from the register.

If the register contains an incorrect entry, the company can be compelled by the court to rectify it. Rectification will be ordered in any appropriate case but this power will not be exercised if injustice will be caused to other members.

An action may be brought against the company in any case where a person has a right to have the register corrected or amended.

On application of an aggrieved person or any member of the company or the company itself, the register of members may be rectified by the court for any of the following reasons:

a) if the name of any person is, without sufficient cause, entered in or omitted from the register; or

b)   if a default is made or an unnecessary delay takes place in entering on the register the fact of any person having ceased to be a member.

Annual Returns

A company having a share capital is required to send to the Registrar of Companies at least once in each year, a return containing a number of prescribed matters[2] including a list of all persons who (on the fourteenth day after the first or only ordinary General Meeting in the year) are members of the company and of all persons who have ceased to be members since the date of the last return or in the case of the first return, on the incorporation of the company. Annual returns are to be kept in a separate part of the register of members.

A copy of the annual return signed by a director or the secretary must be sent to the Registrar of Companies, usually within forty-two days after such meeting.

Failure to file an annual return renders the company and every officer who is in default liable to a fine.

It should be noted that failure to file an annual return may give cause to the Registrar believing that the company is not carrying on business or is not in operation and justifying the Registrar striking off the company from the Register of Companies.

In the case of public companies and private companies which are obliged to file accounts, the annual return is to include a certified copy of the last balance sheet and profit and loss account which was laid before the company in general meeting, including every document required to be annexed thereto and a copy of the certified report of the auditors.

The information contained in an annual return and the annual accounts are potentially the most useful documents which a company has to prepare and make available for registration and inspection.

• SPECIMEN OF ANNUAL RETURNS IN RELATION TO THE SHARES OF A COMPANY (JAMAICA)[3]

Annual Returns of   Limited made up to   19

THE COMPANIES ACT

Address of the registered office of the company Situation of Register of Members

Address of place at which register of members is kept if other than the registered office of the company

SUMMARY OF SHARE CAPITAL AND SHARES

Nominal Share Capital	$
(divided into* shares of	$
(divided into shares of	$
Total number of shares taken up* to the day of	
must agree with the total shown in the list as held by	
existing members).	$
Number of shares issued subject to payment wholly in cash	$
Number of shares issued as fully paid up otherwise than in cash	$
Number of shares issued as partly paid up to the extent of	
per share otherwise than in cash	$
Number of shares (if any) issued at a discount	
Total amount of discount on the issue of shares which has not been written	
off at the date of this Return	
called upon each of shares	$
called upon each of shares	$
called upon each of shares	$
Total amount of calls received, including payments on application	
and allotment	$
Total amount (if any) agreed to be considered as paid on shares	
which have been issued as fully paid up otherwise	
extent of per share otherwise than in cash	$
Total amount of calls unpaid	$
Total amount of the sums (if any) paid by way of commission in	
respect of any shares or debentures or allowed by way of	
discount in respect of any debentures since the date of the	
last Return	$

Total number of shares forfeited $

Total amount paid (if any) on shares forfeited $

Total amount of shares for which share warrants

to bearer are outstanding $

Total amount of share warrants to bearer   Issued $

     issued and surrendered respectively since the date of

      the last Return   Surrendered $

Number of shares comprised in each share warrant to bearer

Indebtedness

Total amount of indebtedness of the company in respect of all mortgages and charges of the kind which are required to be registered with the Registrar of Companies Act

Date   Secretary_____

Particulars of the Directors of _____ at the date of the Annual Return

The Present Christian Name or Names and Surname	Any former Christian Name or Names or Surname	Nationality	Nationality or origin (if other than the present nationality)	Usual Residence Residential Address	Other business occupation (if any) If none, state so.

LIST OF PAST AND PRESENT MEMBERS

List of persons holding shares in _____ limited on the _____ day of _____ 19____ and of persons who have held shares therein at any time since the date of the last return, or (in the case of the first return) of the incorporation of the company, showing their names, addresses and occupations, and an account of the shares so held.

NAMES, ADDRESSES & OCCUPATIONS			ACCOUNT OF SHARES					REMARKS
Christian	Surname	Address	Occupation	Number of shares held by existing Members at date of Return	Particular since the date of share date of who are trans-ferred the last still return			
				BY PERSONS STILL WHO ARE MEMBERS	BY WHO HAVE TO BE PERSONS CEASED MEMBERS			
					Date of Regis-tration	Number	Date of Regis-tration	
					Number			

Delivered for filing by _____ Secretary

A   We certify that the company has not since the date of the last return issued any invitation to the public to subscribe for any shares or debentures of the company or to deposit money for fixed periods or payable on call whether bearing or not bearing interest, and we also certify that to the best of our knowledge and belief since the abovementioned date no person other than the holders, has except in cases provided for in the Fifteenth Schedule, had any interest in any of the company's shares.

Signed _____ Director

Signed _____ Secretary

B   We certify that to the best of our knowledge and belief, subject to the exceptions provided for in the Sixteenth Schedule, no body corporate holds any shares in the company and that this has been the position at all times since the date of incorporation.

Signed _____ Director

Signed _____ Secretary

Notes

1.   One or more books may be used as a register.
2.   Setting out names, addresses and occupation of every shareholder as well as the number of shares held. See p. 126, supra, for specimen form.
3.   See the Fifth Schedule in the Jamaica Companies Act.

CHAPTER 15

Meetings

Meetings of Members

In theory, the general meeting of members has considerable power to make decisions which affect the management of the company. The calling of meetings of members, the right to attend and vote at such meetings and the method of voting are matters that are set out to a large extent by the articles of the company.

In *Sharp* v *Dawes* [1876]), a meeting was defined as "an assembly of people for a lawful purpose" or "the coming together of at least two persons for any lawful purpose". At common law, therefore, one person cannot constitute a meeting even though he holds proxies[1] for several other persons. To this rule, there are exceptions:

(a)   one person may attend a meeting if it is a class meeting and all the shares are held by that person;

(b)   the court may order a general meeting to be held and if only one member is willing to attend the meeting, the court may fix the quorum at one;

(c)   certain statutory provisions may allow for one person to form a quorum at a meeting.

The articles of association always contain provisions as to the meetings of a company[2] and this should be taken into consideration in the holding of meetings.

Meetings of members of a company fall into two broad divisions — general meetings and class meetings. A meeting where all members are entitled to attend is called a "general meeting", whereas a meeting where only one class of members is entitled to attend is called a "class meeting".

The underlying reason for holding meetings is to allow for members to attend, to debate and to vote on matters affecting the affairs of the company. It is the only occasion offered to members to express their views regarding the conduct of the company's affairs.

General Meetings

The members of a company as a body may take decisions affecting the affairs of the company only through a general meeting, unless all the shareholders assent[3]. At general meetings, decisions are taken by members voting on resolutions[4]. There are two kinds of general meetings – annual and extra-ordinary.

Annual General Meetings

Every company is required to hold an annual general meeting in each calendar year. Generally not more than fifteen months may elapse between meetings, except for the first annual general meeting, which may be held within eighteen months of incorporation of the company. The notice calling the meeting must specify the meeting as an annual general meeting[5].

The annual general meeting provides an opportunity for members to question the stewardship of the directors and other officers about the preceding year.

The business usually transacted at an annual general meeting are:

1. declaring a dividend;
2. directors' and auditors' reports, accounts and balance sheet;
3. the election of directors; *and*
4. the appointment of and the fixing of remuneration the auditors.

Other business may be transacted at an annual general meeting but it is usual to convene an extra-ordinary general meeting for these.

Extra-Ordinary General Meetings

All general meetings other than annual general meetings are called extra-ordinary general meetings.

The directors are usually given power in the articles to call an extra-ordinary general meeting whenever they see fit. They will do so if special business of importance requires a meeting of the members.

Directors may also be required to call an extra-ordinary general meeting by a requisition from the members (usually by members holding issued capital and having voting rights).

Requisites of a valid meeting

A meeting can only reach binding decisions if:
- (a) it has been properly convened;
- (b) a quorum is present;
- (c) a chairman presides;
- (d) resolutions are put to the vote.

Convening a Meeting

A meeting must be properly convened to be valid. For this to be so:

(1) the meeting must be called by the directors or those properly authorized to do so.

The articles usually expressly empower the board of directors to convene general meetings. In any event the common law gives the board this power.

If a general meeting is called by someone other than the directors, e.g. by the secretary, the meeting is void.

The Acts in the Region, however, usually provide that, unless the articles provide to the contrary, two or more members holding not less than one-tenth of the company's issued share capital may request the directors to call a general meeting, in which case the directors must convene an extra-ordinary general meeting. The requisition must state the objects of the meeting and must be signed by the requisitionists. On receipt of a requisition, notice must be given to the members that an extraordinary general meeting is to be held on a date not more than twenty-eight days after the date of the notice.

Members, other than the requisitionists, have no right to have resolutions put on the agenda, but the directors may do so.

If the directors do not convene the meeting within the required period, the requisitionists themselves may convene a meeting within three months of depositing the requisition. Any reasonable expenses incurred by the requisitionists for convening the meeting may be recovered from the company.

The court is normally given statutory power to call a meeting on the application of a director or member.

(2) A meeting cannot be held unless proper notice has been given. Notice must be given to every member whether he is entitled to attend and to vote or not.

The underlying reason for proper notice is that if a member is to be bound by a decision taken at a meeting, he must he given a reasonable opportunity to attend in person so as to debate and to vote on matters arising.

Modern articles usually provide that the accidental omission to give notice to a member or his failure to receive it shall not invalidate the proceedings of the meeting.

The number of days' notice required is to be calculated by excluding the day on which the notice is given and the day on which the meeting is to be held, i.e. clear days.

It is normally provided that an annual general meeting may be held even if less than the required twenty-one days' notice is given, if all the members entitled to attend and vote agree. Any other general meeting may be held even though a shorter notice is given, if accepted as sufficient by a majority of the members entitled to attend and to vote and who between them hold at least ninety-five percent of shares carrying voting rights.

In certain cases special notice is necessary to pass a resolution. This means that a person who intends to move a special resolution to be passed at a general meeting must give *twenty-eight days' notice* to the company of it and the company must give twenty-one days' notice of it to the members at the same time notice of the meeting is given. Special notice is normally required to remove a director or an auditor.

(3)   A notice calling a meeting:

   (a)   must state the time and place at which the meeting will be held;

   (b)   if the meeting is an annual general meeting, it must describe it as such;

   (c)   if the meeting is called to pass a special or extraordinary resolution, it must say so; and the proposed resolution must be set out verbatim;

   (d)   the notice calling a meeting must specify the nature of the business to be transacted at the meeting in sufficient detail to enable members to decide whether they should attend or not, in order to protect their interests. It must be free from anything calculated to confuse or mislead and must be sufficient to enable a member to exercise an informed judgement;

   (e)   a meeting must not be convened at an unreasonable hour or at an inconvenient place nor with the intention of making it impossible for certain members to attend.

At common law, notice of meetings may be excused if the member is beyond summoning distance or if he is too unwell to attend. In the case of registered companies the common law rule does not apply as the Companies Acts allow members to appoint "proxies" to attend the meeting and to vote on their behalf in which case notice should be given.

In every notice calling a meeting of a company, there must appear with reasonable prominence, a section which states that a member who is entitled to attend and to vote can appoint a proxy[6] to attend and to vote on his behalf and that a proxy need not be a member of the company.

Class Meetings

Generally speaking, only the holders of shares to which the class meeting relates should be present at such meetings – Carruth v *ICI* [1937] AC 707.

Quorum

A meeting cannot proceed to business unless a quorum of members is present. A quorum is the minimum number of persons whose presence is necessary for the transactions at the meeting to be valid.

The legislation usually provide for a number of members to be present to form a quorum, unless the articles provide otherwise. Two members present for a private company and three members present for a public company generally constitute a quorum at a general meeting. Members who cannot vote do not count toward a quorum. Proxies also do not count unless the articles provide for this.

Table A provides that two members present in person or by proxy shall constitute a quorum at a general meeting.

If it is provided that a quorum is to be present "at the time when the meeting proceeds to do business", then the court may hold that a quorum need be present only when the meeting commences" – *Re Hartley Baird Ltd.* [1955].

The articles usually provide that if a quorum is not present at a general meeting within half an hour from the time appointed for holding the meeting, it shall stand adjourned until the same time the next week.

Chairman

If the articles make no provision for the appointment of a chairman to preside at a meeting, the members may elect one of their own number to preside at the meeting.

Usually, however, the articles provide that the chairman of the board of directors shall be the chairman of a general meeting or if he fails to attend, or is unwilling to act, that one of the other directors chosen by the directors shall be chairman or if none is present at the meeting any member elected by the members present at the meeting may be chairman.

The chairman's function is to preserve order at the meeting, to call on members to speak, and to take the vote on a resolution. Provision is normally made for the chairman, with the consent of the meeting or at its direction, to adjourn the meeting.

The chairman has authority to decide all incidental questions arising at the meeting concerning its proceedings which call for decisions to be taken at the time. The burden, therefore, is on a person challenging a decision to show that it was wrongly taken.

Duties of Chairman of Meeting of Company

The chairman's position is a very important one. In pursuing his duties he must:

(a) act bona fide in the interests of the company as a whole;
(b) ensure that the meeting is properly convened;
(c) ensure that provisions of the Act and the company's articles are complied with;
(d) preserve order;
(e) put resolutions or motions in their proper form;
(f) exercise his casting vote (if he has one) bona fide in the interests of the company;
(g) exercise his powers of adjournment and demanding of a poll correctly.

Resolutions

Decisions of a meeting are made by passing resolutions.

Any resolution mentioned in the notice calling the meeting may be moved on a motion by a member.

If the resolution for which the meeting was called, is one which must be set out verbatim in the notice, a member cannot move an alternative resolution, otherwise he can.

When a resolution is moved any member may speak on it or move an amendment to it.

In the case of special resolutions or extra-ordinary resolutions any amendment that alters the resolution in substance or effect would be invalid unless proper notice of the amendment was given.

In *Re Moorgate Mercantile Holdings Limited* [1980], it was held that "there must be absolute identity at least in substance, between the notice and the resolution actually passed".

A proxy cannot move a resolution or an amendment or speak on it unless the articles so provide or he has been given a statutory right to do so.

Motions for the closure of discussion on a resolution or the dissolution or adjournment of a meeting may be passed by an ordinary resolution unless the articles otherwise provide.

A proxy appointed to vote on a substantive resolution may vote on these motions.

Kinds of Resolutions

There are three kinds of resolutions which may be passed at a general meeting – special, extra-ordinary and ordinary.

The nature of business to be transacted will determine the kind of resolution to be passed. Generally, an ordinary resolution is sufficient for a decision.

The Companies Act commonly provides that certain things are to be done by special or extra-ordinary resolutions only[7]. Matters not provided for may be dealt with by ordinary resolutions except where the memorandum or articles provide otherwise.

(1) A special resolution is one passed by a majority of not less than three-fourths of the members who are entitled to vote and who voted at a general meeting of which not less than twenty-one days' notice, specifying the intention to propose the resolution as a special resolution was duly given.

To be valid the resolution passed at the meeting must be the same as that specified in the notice, both in form and substance.

A special resolution is required *inter alia* to alter the objects clause of the memorandum or alter the articles or to change the name of the company.

(2) An extra-ordinary resolution is a special resolution save that the notice calling the meeting must state that it is proposed to

pass an extra-ordinary resolution and not less than fourteen days' notice is to be given.

(3) An ordinary resolution is a resolution of which not less than fourteen days' notice is given and which is passed by a simple majority of the votes cast at the meeting.

CARICOM Report

The *CARICOM Report* recommended that:

(i) The following changes are to be regarded as fundamental changes requiring a special resolution:

    (a) change of the company's name or the situation of the registered office;

    (b) alteration of class rights;

    (c) restrictions on share transfers;

    (d) number of directors;

    (e) restriction on powers;

    (f) any other matters which are not intrinsic changes requiring an ordinary resolution.

(ii) The following changes of the articles are to be regarded as intrinsic changes only requiring an ordinary resolution:

    (a) creating a new class of shares;

    (b) increasing the maximum number of shares;

    (c) alterations in share capital (other than reductions of capital or involving alterations of class rights);

    (d) subdivision of shares.

Guyana has adopted the recommendations of the *CARICOM Report*. (See section 5 (4) and Fourth Schedule of the Guyana Companies Act 1991.)

In the case of Barbados, a special resolution is required in all cases (see section 197 of the Barbados Companies Act).

Voting

The general principle is that every member of a company has a right to vote at a general meeting of the company.

The articles usually contain special provisions as to voting at meetings[8].

Generally, a shareholder may exercise the right to vote as he pleases and does not have any duty to take into account the interests of the company or other persons. See *Pender* v *Lushington* [1877]. In *Carruth* v *ICI Industries Limited* [1937] AC 707, it was said that the shareholder's vote is a right of property and may be exercised by the shareholder as he thinks fit in his own interest.

There are two accepted methods of voting – a show of hands and a poll.

- **1. Show of Hands**

  Votes on a resolution are usually taken in the first place by a show of hands. In this case each member present has one vote only, irrespective of the number of shares he holds.

  A proxy cannot vote on a show of hands unless the articles provide for this.

  The chairman declares the result. On the declaration of the result on a show of hands, any member or proxy may demand a poll, unless the articles provide otherwise.

- **2. Poll**

  The articles may provide that for a poll to be demanded this must be made by a certain number of members e.g. by at least three members or by members who hold at least one-tenth of the issued paid-up capital.

The rights of members to vote and the number of votes to which they are entitled to, on a demand of a poll, are fixed in the articles of the company. One vote per share is the norm on voting on a poll. Preference shares may carry no voting rights.

It is customary to provide in the articles that in the case of an equality of votes, the chairman is to have a casting vote in addition to any other vote he may have.

Voting on a show of hands have no effect once a poll has been properly demanded. A poll can be demanded without having a vote by a show of hands – *Holmes* v *Keyes* [1959].

On a poll members have the number of votes attached to their shares and the votes may be given either by the member or his proxy. He need not cast all his votes in the same way.

The right to demand a poll is a common law right. Legislation usually provides that this right may not be excluded by the articles of association .

In the case of registered companies, members are given a statutory right to demand a poll on any question except:

(a)   the election of the chairman; or

(b)   the adjournment of the meeting.

Proxies

A member who is entitled to attend and to vote at a meeting has a right to appoint an agent as "proxy" to attend and to vote on his behalf at the meeting. A proxy need not be a member of the company.

If the company is a public one, the member may appoint two or more proxies to vote in respect of different shares held by him or he may appoint two or more proxies in the alternative, so that if the first named proxy fails to vote, the second one may do so.

Every notice calling a meeting of the company must inform members of their right to appoint proxies and that proxies need not be members of the company[9]. If this is omitted, the directors and secretary are liable to a fine but it appears that the meeting is valid.

The articles of association of the company normally provide the form a proxy should take.

The articles may provide that the appointment of a proxy must be received by the company in advance of the meeting (usually forty-eight hours) before the appointment is considered to be valid.

A proxy may vote on a poll but not on a show of hands unless the articles provide otherwise.

A proxy may also speak at a meeting.

A vote by a proxy for "self and proxies" is good for all the votes he represents.

A member who has appointed a proxy may attend the meeting and exercise his vote, if he wishes. This, however, will revoke the proxy.

Proxies may be revoked at any time before they are acted on. They are revoked on the death of the member.

Proceedings at Meetings

Unless the articles[10] provide otherwise, all members of a company are entitled to attend a general meeting.

Minutes

Every company must keep minutes of its general meetings. The minutes are prima facie evidence of the proceedings at the meeting.

If the minutes are signed by the chairman of the meeting or by the chairman of the next succeeding meeting, it is presumed that the meeting was duly convened and that the proceedings recorded in the minutes were properly taken.

The minutes of general meetings are to be kept at the registered office of the company and members can inspect them free of charge.

Irregularities and Unanimous Assent of the Members

If all the members entitled to attend a general meeting do so and vote unanimously in favour of a resolution[11] without the meeting being properly convened, they are taken to waive any irregularities and the resolution is effective as if it was duly passed at a properly convened meeting – *Re Duomatic* [1969].

In *Cane v Jones* [1980] 1 ALLER 533 it was held that the unanimous consent of the shareholders of a company is equivalent to the passing of a special or extra-ordinary resolution and has the same effect.

In *Re Pearce Duff and Company Limited* [1960] 3 ALLER 222, it was held that if a general meeting was held to pass a special or extra-ordinary resolution but there is some defect in convening or holding it, the resolution will be treated as validly passed if all members entitled to attend the meeting subsequently agree to treat it as binding.

The principle of unanimous assent is effective only if the shareholders assented to a matter which is intra vires the objects of the company though beyond the powers of the directors.

Where all the members are also directors of the company, the directors' meetings will be considered members' meetings.

Table A provides that a resolution in writing signed by *all* members entitled to vote at a general meeting shall be as effective as a resolution passed at a duly convened meeting.

Filing of Resolutions

Special and extra-ordinary resolutions are to be filed with the Registrar of Companies. Once filed they become public documents and persons dealing with the company are deemed to have constructive notice of their contents.

SPECIMEN

Notice of Annual General Meeting

X COMPANY LIMITED

NOTICE OF MEETING

NOTICE IS HEREBY GIVEN that the FIFTY-FIRST ANNUAL GENERAL MEETING of the Company will be held at   on Monday, 9 July 199 at 11:30 am for the purpose of transacting the following business:

1   To receive and consider the Directors' Report, the Auditors' Report and the Audited Accounts for the year ended 31 December 199 ;
2   To elect Directors;
3   To fix the remuneration of Directors;
4   To appoint Auditors and authorize the Directors to fix their remuneration and expenses for the ensuing year;
5   Special Business

As Special Business, to consider the Directors' recommendations and, if deemed fit, to pass the following resolutions as ORDINARY RESOLUTIONS:

RESOLUTION NO. 1 - CAPITAL DISTRIBUTION

"THAT the Company pay a capital distribution of ten cents (10c) per Ordinary Stock Unit, less transfer tax, to stockholders on record as at 31 July 199 .

RESOLUTION NO. 2 - CONVERSION OF SHARES
INTO STOCK UNITS

"WHEREAS by virtue of the provisions of Article 40 of the Articles of Association of Company Limited, and Section 61 of the Companies Act, the Company may by Ordinary Resolution convert any paid up shares into stock; AND WHEREAS for administrative and other attendant conveniences it is expedient that such conversion be made;

BE IT RESOLVED that the five million, one hundred and twenty-eight thousand nine hundred and eleven issued and fully paid ordinary shares of ONE DOLLAR ($1.00) each in the capital of the Company be converted into five million, one hundred and twenty-eight thousand, nine hundred and eleven issued and fully paid ordinary stock units of ONE DOLLAR ($1.00) each".

6   To transact any other business which may properly be transacted at an ordinary general meeting.

DATED this 15 day of June, 199

by ORDER OF THE BOARD

SECRETARY _____

A member entitled to attend and vote at the meeting is entitled to appoint a proxy to attend and vote instead of him. A proxy need not be a member. Proxy forms must be lodged at the Company's registered office, Kingston, not less than 48 hours before time of the meeting. A form of proxy is enclosed for convenience.

SPECIMEN

FORM OF PROXY

I   of   being a member of Company Limited hereby appoint
_____ or failing him_____
of _____ as my proxy to vote
for me on my behalf at the Annual General Meeting to be held on   July 199
and at any adjournment thereof. As witness my hand this _____ day of
_____ 199

Signature _____

Please indicate with a tick in the spaces below how you wish your votes to be cast.

FOR   AGAINST

RESOLUTION 1   To authorize the payment of a capital distribution
RESOLUTION 2   Conversion of shares into stock units

Note:
1 If the appointer is a corporation, this form must be under its common seal or under the hand of an officer or attorney duly authorized.
2 To be valid this proxy must be lodged with Secretary of the Company, not less than 48 hours before the time appointed for holding the meeting.
A proxy need not be a member of the company.

Notes

1. For proxies see p. 138, infra.
2. See Table A, Articles 45-67, p.62, supra.
3. See *Cane v Jones* (1980), p.139, infra.
4. See pp. 135-136, infra.
5. For specimen notice of annual general meeting, see p.141, infra.
6. For a specimen form of a proxy, see p.143, infra.
7. Copies of these resolutions are to be filed with the Registrar of Companies.
8. See Table A, Articles 60-67, pp.64-65, supra.
9. For specimen notice, see p.141, infra.
10. Modern legislation usually give statutory effect to this principle.
11. Such resolutions are normally referred to as "Round Robin" resolutions.

CHAPTER 16

Majority Rule and Minority Protection

Although many of the functions of the company are delegated to the directors of the company the basic rule under the common law is that of majority rule.

The courts have generally been reluctant to interfere in the domestic affairs of the company. They look on companies as democratic bodies in which the minority must abide by the will of the majority and they will not normally interfere with the internal management of the company if it is acting within its powers as provided in the objects clause of the memorandum. The courts take the view that the majority is best qualified to determine what is in the best interest of the company as a whole.

The final control of the company's affairs rests with the majority members through their control of certain resolutions at general meetings (e.g. by passing an ordinary resolution they could remove the directors or by passing a special resolution they could alter the articles curtailing the powers given to the directors to manage the company's affairs). Control is also placed in the majority by virtue of the *Rule in Foss* v *Harbottle* [1843] and the fact that the directors are required to lay annual accounts before the annual general meeting of the company and can there be called to account for their stewardship.

However, where the directors are also the majority shareholders of the company the minority shareholders may not have any protection against the actions of the directors.

It should be remembered that a company, as principal, can ratify the unauthorized acts of its agents, i.e. the directors, so long as the acts are within the objects clause of the company.

Under the legal doctrine of ratification, the company (i.e. majority shareholders) in general meeting can ratify a breach of duty of a director or the board of directors if it is within the powers of the company i.e. within the objects of the company.

Ratification is a concept borrowed from the law of agency where validity can be given to an act of an agent which was unauthorized. The courts have held that the shareholders, acting as a majority, are the best judges as to how the business of the company is to be run. It is only where it appears that some sinister motive has operated that the court normally interferes.

The wishes of the majority, therefore, generally will prevail over the minority. This can work considerable hardships on the minority. To protect the minority, the courts have held that the controlling majority owe a duty to the company to act bona fide and not to commit a fraud on the minority.

The Rule in Foss v Harbottle (The proper plaintiff rule)

The Rule in *Foss* v *Harbottle* plays s a fundamental part in company law. It illustrates the principle of majority control and minority protection. It has two parts.

- **1. The Proper Plaintiff Principle**

    If a wrong is done to the company then the only proper plaintiff to bring an action to redress the wrong is the company itself and not a shareholder or anyone else;

- **2. The Ratifiability Principle**

    Where the minority's complaint is that some act has been done wrongly, which would nevertheless be lawful if there were an ordinary resolution in general meeting to authorize it, then the court will not interfere at the instance of the minority.

The Rule places the majority members in a very strong position over the minority.

In *Bamford* v *Bamford* [1970] Ch 212, Lord Justice Russell said:

> "It would be for the company to decide whether to institute proceedings to avoid the voidable allotment; and again this decision would be one for the company in general meeting to decide by ordinary resolution. To litigate or not to litigate, apart from very special circumstances, is for decision by such a resolution."

In *Foss* v *Harbottle* [1843] two members brought an action against the directors of a company to compel them to make good a loss suffered by the company as a result of the directors selling their own land to the company at more than it was worth. It was held that the action failed. The wrong was done to the company and there was nothing to stop the company taking action if it chose to do so. The action brought by the members, therefore, failed.

A more recent example of the rule occurred in *Pavlides* v *Jenson* [1956] where the directors sold an asset of the company to a third party at a gross undervaluation. A minority shareholder commenced an action to set aside transaction. It was held that he could not do so, for it was up to the company to decide whether to sue the directors for negligence. Alternatively, the company could decide to exonerate them by ratifying their action.

The Rule has resulted from a refusal of the courts to interfere in the management of a company at the instance of a minority of the members who may be dissatisfied with the way the affairs of the company are being conducted by the directors or the majority.

In *Foss* v *Harbottle* [1843], the Vice Chancellor Sir James Wigram said:

> "It was not, nor could it successfully be, argued that it was a matter of course for any individual members of a corporation thus to assume to themselves the right of suing in the name of the corporation. In law the corporation and the aggregate members of the corporation are not the same thing for purposes like this; and the only question can be whether the facts alleged in this case justify a departure from the rule which, prima facie, would require that the corporation should sue in its own name and in its corporate character, or in the name of someone whom the law has appointed to be its representative."

The Rule has the advantage of avoiding multiple actions being brought by all those members who feel aggrieved by a particular action of the management. Disputes among members should be settled by the members themselves in general meeting where the majority should prevail.

It has been said that it is not the court's function to take management's decisions and to substitute its own opinions for those of the directors or the majority. The court's function is to determine questions of law not questions of business.

If the officers of the company are overstepping their authority it is a waste of time for the court to interfere if a general meeting can be called and the unauthorized act is ratified.

It is to be noted that the Rule in *Foss* v *Harbottle* only applies where the majority can cure the irregularity or illegality complained of by passing an ordinary resolution. The courts will interfere at the instance of the minority when this cannot be done, e.g. where the act complained of is ultra vires the company or can only be authorized by a special or extra-ordinary resolution.

Both the common law and statute recognized that majority rule had to be balanced with minority protection and a number of exceptions have been developed to mitigate the harshness of the Rule. The exceptions cover the following:

(a) where the actions cannot be put right by the company in general meeting because they are not ratifiable being ultra vires or illegal;

(b) where the company is unable to take action because those who perpetuated the wrong are in control of the company and they would not pursue an action to remedy the wrong.

Exceptions to the Rule in Foss v Harbottle

• Ultra Vires and Illegal Acts

A minority member is allowed to apply to the court to restrain the commission of an ultra vires or illegal act.

In *Parke* v *Daily News* [1962] 2 ALLER 929 Ch 927, the *Daily News* sold a significant part of its business and proposed to distribute the money received to employees who would be made redundant by the sale. Although most shareholders supported this distribution, the plaintiff (who was also a shareholder) objected. The question was whether the majority vote in favour of the distribution entitled the directors to give away the money of the company (and thus, money would eventually be returned to shareholders, including Mr Parke). The court held that such an action could only be justified if the company would benefit from the distribution. As the company had sold the main part of its business, the kindness to employees could not be justified as having any future effect in securing loyalty or attracting good staff. The distribution was held to be invalid despite the majority vote in favour. Plowman J said:

"We must go back to the root of things. The money which is going to be spent is not the money of the majority. That is clear. It is the money of the company, and the majority want to spend it. What would be the natural limit of their power to do so? They can only spend money which is not theirs but the company's if they are spending it for the purposes which are reasonably incidental to the carrying on of the business of the company. That is the general test. Bona fides cannot be the sole test, otherwise you might have a lunatic conducting the affairs of the company and paying away its money with both hands in a manner perfectly bona fide yet perfectly irrational ... one must ask oneself what is the general law about gratuitous payments which are made by the directors or by a company so as to bind dissentients. It seems to me you cannot say the company has only got power to spend the money which it is bound to pay according to law, otherwise the wheels of business would stop, nor can you say that directors ... are always to be limited to the strictest possible view of what the obligations of the company are. They are not to keep their pockets buttoned up and defy the world unless they are liable in a way which would be enforced at law or in equity. Most businesses require liberal dealings. The test there again is not whether it is bona fide, but whether, as well as being done bona fide, it is done within the ordinary scope of the company's business, and whether it is reasonably incidental to the carrying on of the company's business for the company's benefit."

In *Daniels* v *Daniels* [1978] Ch 406, a husband and wife were the two directors of a company and also the majority shareholders. They caused the company to sell to the wife land owned by the company.

Four years later she sold the land for over twenty-eight times what she had paid for it. The judge permitted minority shareholders to claim against the directors. He said:

> "A minority shareholder who has no other remedy may sue where directors use their powers, intentionally or un-intentionally, fraudulently or negligently, in a manner which benefits themselves at the expense of the company".

Where the Majority is Committing a Fraud on the Minority

"Fraud" in this context has a wider meaning than deceit in the criminal law sense. The question is whether the majority have exercised their powers for a proper corporate purpose or have they misused or abused their power so as to give the majority an advantage over the minority. Various categories have been identified:

    (a)   expropriation of company's property;
    (b)   breaches of duty;
    (c)   acts which benefits the majority at the expense of the company;
    (d)   use of powers for an improper purpose.

Expropriation of Company's Property

In *Meiner* v *Hooper's Telegraph Works* [1874] LR 9 Ch D 350, a rival company had a controlling interest in the company concerned. They used this controlling interest to settle an impending action between the two companies in their favour. The judge said that the majority had "put something in their pockets" at the expense of the minority. This fell squarely within the fraud on the minority exception and would not be permitted.

In *Cook* v *Deeks* [1916] 1 AC 544, the directors diverted to themselves contracts which they should have taken up on behalf of the company. It was held that directors holding a majority of votes would not be permitted to make a present to themselves.

A case falling on the other side of the line, where the behaviour was held to be mere incidental profit-making by the directors, so that the breach of duty could have been ratified is *Regal Hastings Ltd.* v

Gulliver [1942] 1 ALLER 378. In that case, Regal Hastings Ltd owned a cinema. The directors decided to acquire two cinemas with a view to the sale of the whole concern. They formed a subsidiary company. The owner of the cinemas demanded that the subsidiary should have a paid up capital of $5,000 before he would grant a lease. The directors subscribed for $3,000 of the shares and Regal Hastings for $2,000. The concern was then sold and the directors ultimately made a profit on their shares. As this had involved making a profit out of the fiduciary relationship in which they stood to the company, they were bound to repay the profits they had made to the company. However, their action was not a fraud on the minority.

Breaches of Duty

Here, as elsewhere, the only clear distinction between breaches of duty which are ratifiable and those which are not lies in the extent to which the behaviour is regarded as villainous. In *Atwool* v *Merryweather* [1867] 5 Eq 464, a company was formed to acquire a mine from Merryweather. In fact, the mine was worthless and the formation of the company and its subsequent flotation was nothing more than a conspiracy to defraud the public. It was held that the company could get back the money it had paid for the worthless mine, despite the fact that the majority had voted against this course of action.

Acts which benefit a director

In *Daniels* v *Daniels* [1978] Ch 406, the court held that a minority shareholder who has no other remedy may sue where directors use their powers intentionally or unintentionally, fraudulently or negligently in a manner which benefits themselves at the expense of the company.

This case shows that benefit to themselves provides a dividing line between ratifiable and non-ratifiable actions, because it was held in *Pavlides* v *Jensen* [1956] Ch 565 that an individual plaintiff would not be permitted to sue where the claim was based on negligence alone. No exception to the rule in *Foss* v *Harbottle* would be made in such a case.

Use of powers for an improper purpose

Clear instances of actions that are not ratifiable occur where powers given to the directors for one purpose are misused. An example of this is when shares are issued to fend off a take-over or otherwise to alter the balance of voting power within a company. The courts have held that the power to issue shares must only be used where the primary purpose of the issue is to raise capital (*Bamford* v *Bamford* [1970] Ch 212).

In *Sidebottom* v *Kershaw, Leese* [1920], it was held that the expropriation of a competing member's interest by means of a compulsory acquisition of his shares is valid, since it is for the benefit of the company as a whole but a bare power of expulsion is not acceptable.

In *Dafen Tinplate & Co. Ltd.* v *Llanelly Steel* [1920] P was a member of D and used to purchase steel from them. When P started to purchase steel elsewhere a new article was inserted which conferred on the majority an unrestricted power to buy out any shareholders they might think proper. It was *held* that this was a mere power of expulsion and as such went further than was necessary to protect the company's interests.

In *Clemens* v *Clemens Bros. Ltd.* [1976] where the issue reduced the plaintiff's holding from forty-five percent to twenty-four and one half percent, thus removing the power to defeat a special resolution, it was held to be a fraud on the minority as the issue was intended to halve the minority.

In *Baille* v *Oriental Telephone Co.* [1915] a company was successfully restrained from acting on a special resolution of which inadequate notice had been given.

Statutory Remedies for Minority Protection

(i) Just and Equitable

The usual statutory remedy available to minority shareholders who complain of the conduct of majority shareholders, is to seek the winding-up of the company on the ground that it is just and equitable to do so. This power is contained in all regional legislation. In practice however, this power is rarely invoked as it may not be desirable to bring an end to the company.

(ii) Oppressive Conduct

An alternative remedy, which was introduced in the United Kingdom in 1947, was adopted by Jamaica in that country's Companies Act of 1965. Section 196 of that Act provides that any member who complains that the affairs of a company are being conducted in a manner oppressive to some part of the members (including himself) may petition the court for an order under the section and the court has the power to make such an order as it thinks fit to bring an end to the matters complained of including an order regulating the conduct of the companies affairs or an order for the shares of the member to be purchased by the other members or by the company. The courts can only exercise the jurisdiction under the section if the requirements stated therein are satisfied.

"Oppressive" conduct has been the subject of judicial interpretation. In *Scottish C W S Ltd.* v *Meyer* [1959] AC 324, it was said to mean that the company had to exercise its authority "in a manner burdensome, harsh and wrongful". In *Re Lundie Brothers Ltd.* [1965] 1 WLR 1051, it was said that oppressive conduct must indicate some lack of probity or fair dealing towards one or more members of the company.

In *Aubert* v *Pederson* [1975] 13 JLR 155 (a Jamaican Court of Appeal Case), the petitioner was the Managing Director of Golf Beach Inn Hotel. He was dismissed and brought a petition under section 196 on the basis that the action of the respondent in removing him from office and excluding him from management constituted oppressive conduct. It was held that the matters complained of affected him as Managing Director and not as a member and the remedy under section 196 was therefore not available to him.

(iii) Inspection and Investigations

See chapter 24 for appointment of inspectors to investigate the affairs of the company.

Barbados (ss 228 - 231), the Bahamas (ss 287 - 290) and Guyana (ss 224 - 227) have more extensive provisions dealing with the restraining of oppression on the part of the company. The provisions in these territories under their recent legislation are similar and provide that an application may be made to the court to restrain, inter alia:

> "Any act or omission of the company or any of its affiliates, that is oppressive or unfairly disregards the interests of any shareholder or debenture holder, creditor, director or officer of the company and the court may make an order as it thinks fit to rectify the matter complained of".

Proceedings in Relation to the Company

The company, being a legal person in itself, can sue and be sued in its corporate name. Consequently, a company can be sued for a wrong committed by it by anyone, including a member, who has been wronged by the company's action.

The memorandum and the articles of a company constitute a contract between the shareholders and the company and between the shareholders. For example, in *Wood* v *Odessa Waterworks Co.* [1889] a member sued the company for the payment of a dividend payable and in *Pender* v *Lushington* [1877] a member successfully sued the company as he was denied his right to vote by the actions of the shareholders.

There are three forms of action that may be brought by a shareholder:

1. Personal Action
2. Representative Action
3. Derivative Action

In 2 and 3 above, the shareholder normally does not sue in his own name only but sues either:

(i)   in a representative capacity, i.e. he sues for all members (including himself) affected by the breach for relief against the other members of the company; or

(ii) in a derivative capacity, i.e. the member seeks a remedy from a third party on the company's behalf. It is usual to join with the third party, the company as a defendant, to allow the judge to award the company a remedy.

Personal Actions of a Member

A member can always bring an action against the company for a wrong done to him in his capacity as a member. In this case he may sue in his own name to enforce his rights against the company (*Pender* v *Lushington* [1877]).

The rights of a member arise in part from the contract between the company and himself which is implied, on his becoming a member and, in part, under the general law. For example, a member is entitled to have his name and shareholding entered on the register of members; to vote at meetings; to receive dividends which have been duly declared; to have his capital returned in accordance with the priority rules on winding up.

Under the general law, a member is entitled to restrain the company from doing acts which are ultra vires; to have an opportunity to speak at meetings; to transfer his shares; not to have his financial obligations increased without his consent; and to exercise the many rights conferred on him by the Companies Act.

A distinction should be made against personal rights vested in the member and corporate rights vested in the company by virtue of the Companies Act, the memorandum and the articles.

Representative Action

Representative action is one brought by a member on behalf of himself and other members of the company, who are not made defendants, to enforce rights common to all the members or that class which he represents. They must have the same interest in the proceedings.

A representative action is normally brought to protect the personal rights of the member and those other members represented by the member. The company, the directors and opposing shareholders are normally joined as the defendants.

Derivative Actions

Derivative actions are usually brought to vindicate the company's rights but the directors have majority control and will not allow litigation to be brought in the company's name. The activities complained of are usually committed by the directors, and are not in the company's interests.

In the derivative action a member is allowed to sue on behalf of himself and other members to remedy wrongs done to the company and to enforce company's rights which are being blocked by the directors and the majority. In such proceedings, the practice is to join the company and the wrongdoers as defendants. This results in the company being bound by the judgement in whose name it will be given.

In *Wallersteiner* v *Moir* (No 2) [1975] the Court of Appeal held that the Court had power to order the company to indemnify the plaintiff against the costs incurred in bringing a derivative action, as it is the company which will ultimately benefit from the proceedings. The right to costs however will depend on whether the plaintiff acted in good faith in bringing the proceedings.

(See also *Prudential Assurance* v *Newman Industries Ltd.* [1982].)

CHAPTER 17

Management and Control

Directors

A company, because it is an artificial person, has no physical existence of its own. The management of its affairs therefore is generally entrusted to natural persons who are called "directors". Certain residual power is, however, reserved to the members in general meeting.

Directors are the persons who direct and control the affairs of the company and represent it in its dealings with the outside world. They are the "controlling" or "directing mind and will" of the company. They speak and act for the company and the action of the directors is the action of the company (*Tesco Supermarkets Ltd* v *Nattrass* [1972].

Any person who occupies the position of a director, by whatever name called, is usually considered to be a director. It matters not if the directors are called "board of governors", "board of management", "governing council", "board of directors", or any other similar name. It is the function and not the name that matters.

There is no legal requirement that a natural person must be appointed. Another company may therefore be a director, in which case it will act through a representative.

Together with the secretary of the company and the managers, the directors are the "officers" of the company. Under the various Acts, it is provided that in certain cases both the company and its officers are liable for offences caused by the acts or defaults of the company's officers.

Generally, no special qualification is required to become a director of a company in the Region.

Exercising of the Powers of the Company

The Companies Acts of the Region normally require certain powers to be exercised by the members in general meeting. Subject to this, the powers of the company are divided between the board of directors and members in general meeting as provided by the memorandum and articles of association. The extent of directors' powers is to be found in the articles of the company. (See Table A, Articles 71-75, p. 65, supra.)

The Companies Acts usually require the following powers of the company to be exercised by members in general meeting:

(a) altering the memorandum and articles;
(b) altering the share capital;
(c) removing directors;
(d) appointing auditors;
(e) winding up the company.

In addition, the articles of the company normally reserve for the members in general meeting the following powers:

(i)   fixing the rights to be attached to a new issue of shares;
(ii)   appointing directors;
(iii) declaring dividends;
(iv)   capitalizing profits and reserves.

Powers of Management

It is usual for the articles of the company to provide for the directors "to manage the business of the company and to exercise all the powers of the company except those which the Companies Act and the memorandum and articles require to be exercised by the members in general meeting". (See Table A, Article 71, p 65, supra.)

The distribution of this power can be varied from time to time by an alteration of the memorandum or the articles by special resolutions. However, the articles cannot be altered with retrospective effect to affect acts already done by directors.

The Board's powers can be as broad or as narrow as is desired, but the tendency is to follow Table A.

It is possible for the articles to vest the same power in the members and in the directors concurrently, in which case the members are the supervisory body and their decision would apply above that of the directors.

The articles may also provide that the directors may exercise certain of their powers subject to any directions given by a general meeting by special resolution[1]. In this case the directions must be followed.

Where powers have been vested in the directors generally, the members cannot interfere with their exercise. They simply cannot take over the functions of the directors. A resolution of a majority at a general meeting of a company cannot impose its will upon the directors, if the articles have given the directors the control of the company's affairs. Only the directors acting as a board can exercise the powers vested in the board.

In *John Shaw and Sons (Salford) Ltd.* v *Shaw* [1935], Grier L J said:

> "If the powers of management are vested in the directors they and they alone can exercise those powers. The only way in which the general body of shareholders can control the exercise of the powers vested by the articles in the directors is by altering the articles or by refusing to re-elect the directors of whose action they disapprove. They cannot themselves usurp the power which the articles have vested in the directors more than, the directors can usurp the powers vested, in the general body of shareholders by the articles. "

If the directors act within the powers given to them under the articles, they are not bound to obey resolutions passed by shareholders at a general meeting; such resolutions cannot override a decision of the directors or control the exercise of their powers in the future. Thus a resolution in general meeting requiring the directors to exercise the powers in a particular fashion will be inconsistent with the articles confirming the power *(Scott* v *Scott* [1943]).

In *Howard Smith Ltd.* v *Ampol Petroleum Ltd.* [1974] AC 821, Lord Wilberforce said:

> ". . . it is established that directors, within their management powers, may take decisions against the wishes of the majority of shareholders,and indeed that the majority of shareholders cannot control them in the exercise of these powers while they remain in office."

The general power of management applies only to managing the company as a going concern. It is subject to legislation and the company's memorandum and articles *(Salmon* v *Quin and Axtens Ltd.* [1909] 1 Ch 311).

If for some reason the directors cannot or will not exercise the powers vested in them, the general meeting may do so. Action by the general meeting has been held valid where there was a deadlock of the board, where there were no directors, where a quorum could not be obtained.

A director's acts are valid despite any defect that may afterwards be discovered with respect to his appointment or qualification *(Dawson* v *African Consolidated Land & Trading Co.* [1898].

Appointment of Directors

Every registered company must have a board of directors. The power to appoint directors to the board is normally to be found in the memorandum or the articles of association. The power is to be exercised as so laid down.

In the Region's legislation it is commonly provided that for a private company there must be at least one director and for a public company there must be at least two directors[2].

A sole director is normally prohibited from also being the company secretary.

The articles usually fix the minimum and maximum number of directors for the composition of the board. In practice, the first directors are usually named in the articles of association and the power to appoint subsequent directors is usually exercisable by the members in general meeting by ordinary resolution.

The board of directors is usually empowered to fill casual vacancies. Directors so appointed usually hold office only until the next annual general meeting.

The articles of the company may authorize the appointment of a director for any period and the appointment is valid if made consistent with the articles.

No special qualifications[3] are required for an appointment as a director. On registration of the company, the company must send to the Registrar of Companies particulars of the first directors. In the case of public companies before a director can act as such, he must send to the Registrar a written consent to act. This is not applicable to a private company. Subsequent changes must also be sent to the Registrar. Undischarged bankrupts and persons convicted on indictment for fraud cannot act as directors.

Vacating of the Office of a Director

Whatever the duration of a director's appointment, he ceases to be a director automatically when his period of appointment expires. In addition, if a director becomes disqualified by law or by the articles he automatically vacates his office.

Neither the members nor the board of directors have an inherent power to remove directors before the expiration of their period of appointment. Express power should be given. If the articles do not specify the duration of a director's appointment, he holds office at will and may be dismissed by an ordinary resolution of a general meeting of the members.

The Companies Acts of the Region usually provide that a company has power to remove a director before the end of his period of office by ordinary resolution at a general meeting of which special notice has been given. In this case, a director may be removed despite anything in the articles or the service contract between the company and the director. He may, however, have a cause for action against the company for breach of his service contract, if any, with the company.

If by the articles the shares held by the directors whose removal is sought carry additional or multiple voting rights as compared with the shares of other members, the director may use these rights to defeat the resolution for his removal. In *Bushell v Faith* [1970] 1 ALLER 53, the company's articles contained a provision that if a resolution was proposed to remove a director, each share of the director would carry three votes instead of the usual one. It was held by the House of Lords that such provision in the articles was valid.

If a company is notified that a member intends to move a resolution for the removal of a director, it must inform the director concerned. The director may require the company to circulate a statement of his defence to the members. The director is also entitled to address the meeting at which the resolution is considered.

A director's removal does not prejudice any right he may have to bring an action for damages for wrongful dismissal or to compensation for loss of office *(Southern Foundries (1926) Ltd.* v *Shirlaw* [1940]).

The articles normally provide for the vacating of director's office in certain circumstances, viz.:

(a)   if the appointment is unlawful by virtue of the Act
(b)   if he becomes bankrupt
(c)   if he is of unsound mind
(d)   if he resigns
(e)   if he is absent from board meetings for more than six months without permission.

Remuneration of Directors

A director is not an employee of the company and is not entitled as such to any remuneration for his services, unless this is expressly provided for in the company's articles or the director has a service contract with the company which provides for remuneration. However, the articles may allow the company in general meeting to fix remuneration for the director.

Register of Directors

Every company must keep a register of directors and secretaries. Certain particulars with respect to each director must be stated in the register – particulars such as address, nationality, occupation, date of birth and other directorships. A register of the directors and secretaries of the company must be kept at the registered office. Where the director is a corporate body, the register must give the corporate name and its registered office.

The company must, usually within fourteen days after any change of directors or of the particulars registered with respect to them, send a notice to this effect to the Registrar of Companies.

A director's name is to be shown on every trade catalogue, business letters, circulars and show-cards of the company.

A director who is in any way interested in a contract with the company must declare his interest at a board meeting. His interest must be declared at the first board meeting at which the contract was discussed or at the first meeting after his interest arose.

A register of director's shareholding and debenture holding in the company and debenture holdings must also be kept at the registered office.

Board Meetings

Directors can only exercise their powers collectively by passing resolutions at board meetings, unless the articles provide otherwise[4]. Where the company has only one director that director may constitute a meeting.

However, if all the directors agree informally or acquiesce on a certain matter without a board meeting being held, this is equivalent to a resolution passed by the board and is binding on the company. The articles may provide that such a resolution is to be reduced to writing and signed by all the directors[5].

Proper notice is to be given to all directors in sufficient time to enable them to attend a board meeting. This would depend on the facts at the time the notice was given. Notice of a board meeting need not be in writing. An oral notice will suffice.

Unlike meetings of members, it is not necessary to state in the notice of a directors' meeting what business is to be transacted at the meeting.

Unless the articles provide otherwise, any director can call a meeting of the board at any time, with reasonable notice being given. This may be days, hours, or even minutes, depending on the particular circumstances.

A quorum of directors must be present before the board can proceed to business. Quorums are usually fixed in the articles.

Any quorum must be a disinterested quorum. If the articles disable a director from voting on a particular matter, e.g. because he has a personal interest in it, he does not count towards a quorum.

Unless the articles provide otherwise, each director has one vote except the chairman who is usually given a casting vote by the articles.

If for some reason the directors are unable or unwilling to exercise their powers of management, those powers will revert to and can be exercised by the company in general meeting (Barron v Potter [1914] 1 Ch 895).

Minutes of Board Meetings

Minutes of board meetings must be kept. Directors can inspect the minute book but members do not have this right. When minutes are signed by the chairman, they become prima facie evidence of the proceedings.

Delegation

Unless the Companies Act or the articles provide otherwise, the board cannot delegate its powers to one or more of its members or to others. The articles usually do. The board can, of course, appoint agents and servants of the company.

Directors as Agents

The directors are agents for the company. They are not agents for the members. The members therefore cannot, by a resolution, direct them with respect to the manner in which they should exercise their powers (*Percival* v *Wright* [1902])[6].

Duties of Directors to the Company

Unlike members, directors have a duty to attend to the company's affairs. In doing so, they owe:

 (i) a fiduciary duty to the company similar to those owed by an agent to his principal; and

 (ii) a duty to take reasonable care and skill in the management of the company's affairs.

These duties are owed exclusively to the company.

Fiduciary Duty (trust and confidence)

The law gives directors freedom to exercise the powers assigned to them but they do so as fiduciaries. The fiduciary duty is owed to the company and not to the individual shareholders. In *Percival* v *Wright* [1902] the directors purchased shares from a member without revealing that negotiations were in progress for the sale of all the shares in the company at a higher price. It was held that the directors held no fiduciary duty to the individual member and they were under no duty to inform him of the negotiations.

The fiduciary duty owed by a director is similar to those applying to any other fiduciary, e.g. an agent or a trustee. The duty is based on the principle that since the company places its trust and confidence in the directors they must display the utmost good faith towards the company in their dealings with or on its behalf.

As fiduciaries, directors must not do any act which is *illegal* or ultra vires the company. They must not exceed the powers conferred on them by the articles. They can do nothing which the company cannot do under its memorandum of association, i.e. they cannot act beyond the corporate capacity of the company.

In *Regal (Hastings) Ltd.* v *Gulliver* [1942] the directors of the Regal company formed a subsidiary company to buy two other cinemas so that the three cinemas could be sold together. As the Regal company was unable to provide all the necessary capital the directors purchased some of the shares in the subsidiary so as to enable the transaction to be effected. These shares were later sold at a profit. It was held that the directors were in fiduciary relationship to the company and had to account to the company for the profit made.

Directors must exercise the powers entrusted to them in good faith for the benefit of the company as a whole and for the purposes for which they are conferred.

"Benefit of the company" means that the directors must have regard to the interests of the present and future members of the company, i.e. they must see the company as a going concern[7]. They must not put themselves in a position where their duties to the company are in conflict with their personal interest. In *Boardman* v *Phipps* [1967]. Boardman, a solicitor, and Phipps were trustees of an estate, comprising shares in a private company. They concluded that the position of the company was unsatisfactory and with the knowledge of the other trustees, they endeavoured to obtain control of the company by purchasing shares in their own names. As the trustees were not empowered to invest trust money in the company's shares, Boardman obtained information from the company as to the price at which shares had changed hands by purporting to act on behalf of the trustees. Both made a considerable profit from the capital distributions on the shares. It was held that both had to account for the profit to the beneficiaries. The information relating to the shares and the opportunity for investment came as a result of their appointment as trustees and therefore as fiduciaries.

When considering the benefit of the company, the question of an act being ultra vires the company must be considered (*Re Horsley and Weight Ltd.* [1982]).

Directors must not abuse their powers in order to maintain their control over the company and they must not exercise their powers so as to gain a private advantage or for an improper purpose.

If directors dishonestly use their powers for an improper purpose, they would not have acted bona fide and would have broken their fiduciary duty.

Even though directors may have acted honestly in what they believe to be the best interests of the company, they may still be in breach of their powers if they do not use them for the purposes for which they were conferred. In *Hogg* v *Cramphorn* [1967], in order to prevent a take-over bid which the directors believed would not be in the best interest of the company, the directors issued shares carrying ten votes each to trustees of an employee pension fund. The shares were paid for by the trustees out of an interest-free loan from the company. It was held that the proper purpose of issuing shares is to raise capital for the company. An issue of shares made to forestall a takeover bid was for an improper purpose and the directors were in breach of their fiduciary duty.

It is an improper purpose if shares are issued solely for the purpose of destroying the existing majority. In *Howard Smith* v *Ampol Petroleum Ltd.* [1974], Lord Wilberforce said "it must be unconstitutional for directors to use their fiduciary powers over the shares of the company purely for the purpose of destroying an existing majority or creating a new majority which did not previously exist".

The power to issue shares is in the nature of a trust to enable the directors to raise additional capital or obtain some advantage which will benefit the company. It may not be used to alter the balance of voting power within the company so as to oppress the minority *(Clemens* v *Clemens Bros. Ltd.* [1976]).

The fiduciary duty is owed by each director individually. A director, in exercising his powers, must bring an independent judgement to bear. He will be liable in damages for loss caused to the company where he simply acts under the direction of another person.

In some circumstances, a director will be expected to seek specialist advice and will be liable for loss occasioned by his failure to do so.

In *Re Duomatic Ltd.* [1969] 2 Ch 365, the directors made a payment to a former director as compensation for loss of office without considering whether the director's conduct justified payment. It was held that they acted unreasonably in failing to obtain advice and were liable in negligence to make good the loss to the company.

In *Lournho Ltd.* v *Shell Petroleum Co. Ltd.* [1980], Lord Diplock said that the principle that directors must act in the best interests of the company "are not exclusively those of its shareholders but may include those of its creditors", and in *West Mercia Safetywear Limited* v *Dodd* [1988] BCLC 250, the Court of Appeal held that a director of an insolvent company must have regard to the interests of its creditors.

• Relief from Liability

If the directors exercise a power for a proper purpose and in good faith, their judgement will not be questioned by a court. In *Howard Smith* v *Ampol Petroleum Ltd.* [1974] it was stated:

> "If the directors act within their powers, if they act with such care as is reasonably expected from them, having regard to their knowledge and experience and if they act honestly for the benefit of the company they represent, they discharge their duty to the company".

Directors must manage the company's affairs in accordance with the principles of common law, the Act and the company's memorandum and articles of association.

Directors, like other agents, incur no personal liability on contracts made by them on behalf of the company which is within the scope of their powers.

Except for the managing director, an individual director as such is not an agent of the company. He can become an agent if he is authorized by the board or he is held out by the company as its agent. However, for the company to be bound, the authorization must not be inconsistent with the memorandum and articles of association.

• Holding Out

In *Hely-Hutchinson* v *Brayhead Ltd.* [1967] 3 ALLER 98, R was chairman of Brayhead and acted as its de facto managing director though he was not so appointed. He often entered into large transactions on behalf of the company and sometimes without seeking authority from the board. The board acquiesced in this course of conduct of R. R gave certain guarantees to the bank on behalf of the company. The company later repudiated these guarantees on the ground that R had no authority. Held that as the board acquiesced in R's previous conduct to act as the chief executive of the company, the transaction fell within the authority that would normally be attached to the position and the company was bound.

See also *Freeman and Lockyer* v *Buckhurst Park Properties (Mangal) Ltd.* [1964] 1 ALLER 630 where K, a director, was left in charge to manage the business. He was never appointed to this position. He engaged architects on behalf of the company. Held though K was not appointed, he had apparent authority to bind the company.

It is quite possible for the articles to vest the same powers in the members and directors concurrently, in which case in the event of a conflict, the members' decision would prevail as the members in general meeting are the supervisory authority.

It is to be remembered that the company cannot confer powers on an agent greater than it possesses under its objects clause.

As a fiduciary:

(i)   A director has an obligation not to profit personally from his position as a director and not to allow a conflict to arise between his duty as a director and his personal interests.

(ii) A director is disqualified from usurping for himself or for his own benefit a business opportunity which his company is actively pursuing.

(iii) The liability of a director to account for secret profits does not depend on fraud or absence of bona fides on his part. This liability arises from the mere fact of a profit having been made.

(iv) Deferment of a company's plans does not entitle a director to usurp those plans or business opportunities flowing from them. (A company's property could include information made available to the director by virtue of his being director – information which the company is entitled to and which is valuable to the company and to the use of which the company has a vested interest.)

Duties of Care and Skill

Directors must exercise ordinary care and skill in the performance of their duties as directors and if possessed of special knowledge or experience they must use it in the affairs of the company. The standard however is not unduly burdensome. The degree of skill varies according to the qualifications and knowledge of the director in question. (See *Re City Equitable Fire Insurance Co. Ltd.* [1925]).

Directors will be liable for negligence in the carrying out of their duties, but will escape liability if the damage results to the company because they relied on officers of the company whom they believed to be reliable and competent.

As a general rule under the common law a director will not be held liable for negligence unless guilty of gross or inexcusable negligence in a business sense. In *Re City Equitable Fire Insurance Co. Ltd.* [1925] Ch 407 the following propositions were laid down:

(i) A director need not exhibit in the performance of his duties a greater degree of skill than may reasonably be expected from a person of his knowledge and experience; the director need not have knowledge of the company's business and very little experience. He is not liable for mere errors of judgement, for want of judgement is not negligence.

    (ii) A director is not bound to give continuous attention to the affairs of the company. His duties are of an intermittent nature to be performed at periodic board meetings. This is subject to the appointment of a full time director, e.g. managing director, who is subject to the terms of his contract.

   (iii) A director is, in the absence of suspicion, justified in relying on the officers of the company to carry out their duties honestly. It is generally not a duty of a director, except the managing director, to exercise control over the day to day running of the business.

A director will be liable for a negligent decision to which he was a party, but he will generally not be liable in respect of a decision taken at a meeting at which he was not present. There is some doubt as to how far this rule will apply, for it will not apply to cases when the director has knowledge or notice that a duty which ought to have been performed was not being performed or there is acquiescence on his part. Probably the most important aspect of the standard of care imposed on a director is that he is not required to have any special qualification or any expertise at all in the business in which the company is engaged. In *Re Brazilian Rubber Plantations and Estates Ltd.* [1911] 1 Ch 425, it was stated:

> "A director's duty has been laid down as requiring him to act with such care as is reasonably to be expected from him having regard to his knowledge and experience. He is, I think, not bound to bring any special qualifications to his office. He may under-take the management of a rubber company in complete ignorance incurring responsibility for the mistakes which may result from such ignorance."

Directors' negligence may be ratified by a majority of the members provided there is no fraud on the minority and the act is within the company's objects.

Directors' Contracts with the Company

The effect of contracts made by a director with a company of which he is the director presents considerable difficulty as this may give rise to a conflict of interests and breach of his fiduciary duty.

At common law and in the absence of anything to the contrary in the articles, a director could not safely contract with his company unless a general meeting on full disclosure approved the contract. The director concerned must make full disclosure of his interest, including its extent and the amount of his profit or reward. (See *Industrial Development Consultants* v *Cooley* [1972]).

Recent legislation may allow a director to be a party to a contract with the company, provided there is full disclosure to the directors at a meeting of the directors and approval is given. (See section 188 of the Companies Act of Jamaica and section 89 of the Barbados Companies Act 1982.)

Liability for Acts of Co-Directors

A director is not liable for the acts of his co-directors of which he has no knowledge and in which he has taken no part. If a director is fraudulent his co-directors are not liable in the absence of circumstances to arouse their suspicion.

Competing Directorates

In the absence of a provision to the contrary in the articles of the company or any contract made with a director, a director may accept a directorship in another company though it is in direct competition. He must not, however, use any confidential information which he obtains as a result of his office in one company for the benefit of the other company.

In *Cranleigh Precision Engineering Ltd.* v *Bryant* [1964] 3 ALLER 289 the defendant acquired valuable technical information as the plaintiff's managing director. He subsequently sought to turn this information to his own advantage. The court granted an injunction restraining him from committing a breach of confidence. In *Thomas Marshall (Exports)* v *Guinle* [1979] 1 Ch 222; [1978] 3 ALLER 193, the managing director for his own benefit established a relationship with company's suppliers. Held it was a breach of a fiduciary duty. However, see chapter 21, infra, on insider dealing.

Share Qualifications

A company is not required by law to impose a share qualification for directors. The articles may, however, provide for a director to hold a minimum number of shares in the company. This is to ensure that the director has a material stake in the success of the company and will devote his best endeavours in its service.

Register of Directors' Interests

It is normally provided that a company must keep a register showing the interests of each director in its shares and interests of its holding and subsidiary companies. A director is considered as being interested in shares or debentures in which his spouse or a child has an interest as though the interest was his own.

Loans to Directors

Normally a company, is prohibited from making loans to a director except if the company is in the business of money-lending or, in the case of Jamaica[8], is a private company.

Director's Service Contract

A copy of a director's service contract with the company is normally required to be kept at the registered office or its principal place of business within the territory.

The Managing Director

The managing director of a company is its chief executive officer. The board of directors have no authority to appoint a managing director unless the articles authorize them to do so. The articles usually provide for the board to appoint one of their number as managing director on such terms as the board thinks fit, including that he may be removed at any time by the company in general meeting.

The managing director is normally appointed under a service

contract, setting out his powers and duties and terms of employment. He may exercise the powers conferred on him by the board and by the articles. In the absence of expressed powers, the managing director will have all those powers which are usually given to a managing director. His powers will be actual and apparent as any other agent.

Where a managing director lacks actual authority when dealing with an outsider, the company may still be liable if it has held out to the outsider that the managing director has the necessary authority. He is said to have apparent authority to enter into the contracts with third parties (*Freeman & Lockyer* v *Buckhurst Park Properties (Mangal) Ltd.* [1964] 2 QB 480; *Hely-Hutchinson* v *Brayhead Ltd.* [1968] 1 QB 549).

A managing director, during his term of office, is not subject to retirement by rotation but his appointment may be terminated if his appointment is revoked by the board of directors or if he ceases to be a director.

If there is a breach of his service contract he may be entitled to bring an action for damages for such breach. This is independent of the articles, for a company is entitled to alter its articles at any time. The articles do not themselves form a contract between the company and the managing director as is the case with a member.

The managing director is in a different position to an ordinary director. He holds two positions – that of a director and that of a manager. He exercises a wide range of executive functions and is normally responsible for the day to day running of the company. He is the most single important figure in the management of the company. He is not a "servant" of the company for the purpose of receiving preferential payment of his salary on a winding-up of the company. (See *Read* v *Astoria Garage (Streatham) Ltd* [1952].)

In *Southern Foundries (1926) Ltd.* v *Shirlaw* [1940] it was held that a managing director's service contract contained an implied condition that the company would not make it impossible for him to carry out his duties.

Committees of Directors

The articles of a company usually permit the directors to delegate any of their powers to a committee of the directors subject to such conditions as the directors may impose.

The power to delegate to a committee must not be used as a device to exclude a particular director from the management of the company.

The Secretary of the Company

The Region's legislation commonly provides that every company must have a secretary but a sole director cannot, also, be the secretary.

The secretary is usually appointed by the directors on such terms as they think fit. The directors can also remove the secretary. The articles of the company usually have provisions to this effect.

The first secretary of a company is normally appointed by the subscribers of the memorandum of association.

At one time, the secretary was considered to be a mere servant whose position was to carry out the directions of the board of directors. He himself had no authority to bind the company merely by being the secretary of the company.

In *Barnett Hoares & Co.* v *South London Tramways* [1887], Lord Esher MR had this to say about the secretary:

> "A secretary is a mere servant; his position is to do what he was told and no person can assume that he has authority to represent anything at all."

Today the position is no longer so, as was pointed out by Lord Denning MR in *Panorama Developments (Guildford) Ltd.* v *Fidelis Furnishing Fabrics Ltd.* [1971]:

> "Times have changed. A company secretary is a much more important person nowadays than he was in 1887. He is an officer of the company with extensive duties and responsibilities. He is no longer a mere clerk. He is certainly entitled to sign contracts connected with the administrative side of a company's affairs such as employing staff and ordering cars and so forth".

Today, the company's secretary is the administrative officer of the company and duties would include:

(a)   ensuring that the company's records are in order;

(b)   ensuring that the requisite returns are filed with the Registrar of Companies;

(c)   ensuring that the company's registers are properly maintained;

(d)   taking minutes at meetings;

(e)   sending out notices; and

(f) countersigning documents to which the company's seal is affixed.

In addition, a company secretary has implied authority to make certain contracts on behalf of the company in relation to his duties, e.g. contracts such as employing office staff and the purchasing of office equipment and stationery.

However, this authority, unless expressly given, does not extend to matters such as:

(i) binding the company on a commercial contract;

(ii) borrowing money on behalf of the company;

(iii) registering a transfer of shares;

(iv) striking a name off the register of members;

(v) summoning a general meeting on his own authority;

(vi) issuing a writ or filing a defence in the company's name.

In the Companies Act (1982) of Barbados, section 58 (2) provides that the directors of a public company must take all reasonable steps to ensure that the secretary or each joint secretary is a person who appears to the directors to have the requisite knowledge and experience to discharge the functions of a secretary of a public company.

Notes

1. See pp. 133-134, supra.
2. In Barbados a public company must have at least three directors, two of whom must not be officers or employees of the company or its affiliates – (s 59).
3. In Barbados an individual who is less than 18 years of age, or is of unsound mind or a bankrupt cannot be a director (s 63). In addition, on application of the Registrar, the court may disqualify a director if he is unfit to be concerned in the management of a public company – (s 64).
4. In recent legislation, provision is made for a director to participate in a board meeting by telephone or other communication facilities – (section 79 of Barbados Act 1982).
5. Such resolutions are referred to as "Round Robin" resolutions.
6. See, e.g., s 80 of the Barbados Act 1982.
7. *Gaiman v National Association from Mental Health* [1971] ch 317.
8. See s. 179 of the Jamaica Companies Act.

CHAPTER 18

Auditors

The independent examination of the company's accounts by a person of established competence is regarded as an indispensable feature of company practice.

In the Region, in some territories, some provisions are made in relation to the appointment of auditors. However, legislation in some of the territories is largely absent, leaving these matters to be dealt with in the articles. The modern trend is to lay down a set of rules which set out the qualifications, the method of appointment and replacement and the powers and duties of auditors.

Qualification of Auditors

Before a company appoints an auditor, it must be ensured that the person is qualified for appointment. In older legislation, no special qualification is required. In the more recent legislation, this is not so. For example, in Jamaica, for a company required to file accounts with the Registrar, an auditor must be a registered public accountant; in Barbados he must be a member of the Institute of Chartered Accountants; and in the Bahamas he must be a professionally qualified auditor or an accountant licensed to practise as such.

Disqualification

Whilst qualifications may not have been specifically prescribed, it is usual to find some disqualifications laid down in the legislation. The following persons are usually disqualified:

(a) any officer or servant of the company or an associated company;

(b) any partner or employee of such an officer or servant;

(c) any corporate body.

In addition, in the Barbados (s 154) and Bahamas (s. 132) provisions, a partner in an accounting or auditing firm is disqualified from being appointed an auditor of a company in which any other partner of his firm is an officer or employee of the company.

Appointment

The first auditors are usually appointed by the directors before the first annual general meeting is held, as in the case of Jamaica and Trinidad and Tobago, or the statutory meeting for other countries in the Region. If they fail to do so, the company in general meeting, may appoint the first auditors.

Under the usual provisions found in the Region's legislation, the general rule is that at each annual general meeting, the company must appoint an auditor or auditors to hold office from the conclusion of that meeting to the conclusion of the next annual general meeting. The directors have the power to fill casual vacancies.

A retiring auditor may be re-appointed without any resolution being passed. In Jamaica special notice is required for a resolution to appoint a person other than a retiring auditor (s 153).

Remuneration

Remuneration is generally fixed by the company at the annual general meeting in such manner as the company in general meeting may determine. Few companies fix remuneration at the general meeting. Instead, they authorize the directors to fix the remuneration which can then be related to the actual work involved in auditing the accounts. A suitable resolution is included in the minutes of the annual general meeting allowing for this.

Removal

The company may by ordinary resolution remove an auditor before the expiration of the period of his appointment despite any agreement between the company and himself. Special notice is required to be given of the resolution in the case of Jamaica.

A retiring auditor may be re-appointed without any resolution being passed unless he is not qualified or a resolution has been passed at the general meeting that he should not be re-appointed or he has given notice in writing of his unwillingness to be re-appointed.

Resignation

The general practice is that a resigning auditor maintains his silence on the reasons for vacating office.

In Barbados and Guyana, there are provisions reflecting the recommendations of the *CARICOM Report*, to the effect that:

(a)   where an auditor resigns he is required to give a statement of any circumstances connected with the company which should be brought to the attention of the members or creditors or if there are no such circumstances, a statement to that effect;

(b)   where he gives a statement of such circumstances, the auditor should be permitted to requisition a general meeting to explain the statement;

(c)   the auditor should be given a right to attend, and be heard at any such meeting.

Duties of Auditors

Not in all cases does regional legislation deal specifically with auditors' duties. In such cases, the matter is left to be dealt with by the company's articles, the common law and the practice of the accounting profession.

In modern legislation, the auditors' principal duty is to make a report to the members of the company on the accounts examined by them and on every balance sheet, every profit and loss account and all group accounts laid before the company. (See, for example, the Jamaica's Companies Act, Section 156 and the Tenth Schedule.)

Certain matters are required to be expressly stated in the auditors' report. For example:

(a) whether, in their opinion, the company's balance sheet and profit and loss account in the case of individual accounts, and in the case of a holding company the group accounts have been properly prepared;

(b) whether, in their opinion, a *true and fair* view is given in the case of group accounts of the state of affairs and the profit and loss of the company and its subsidiaries, dealt with thereby, so far as concerns members of the company.

Auditor's Report

In preparing their report, the auditors are required to carry out such investigations as will enable them to form an opinion as to whether:

(i) proper books of accounts have been kept by the company and adequate returns have been received from branches not visited by them;

(ii) the company's balance sheet and profit and loss account are in agreement with the books of accounts and returns.

If they think that this is not the case they must state that fact in their report.

Auditors are not responsible for matters that are concealed from them but they have a duty to investigate matters if there are grounds for suspicion – *Re Kingston Cotton Mill Co. Ltd.* (No 2) [1986].

The auditors have powers which give them the right of access to the company's books, accounts and vouchers as well as the minutes of board meetings.

The auditors may require from the officers of the company any information and explanations which they think necessary and if they fail to obtain these, they must state this fact in their report.

When preparing their report, the auditors must consider whether the information given in the directors' report is consistent with the accounts. If they think that it is not so, they must state that fact in their report.

It is a criminal offence for any officer of a company knowingly or recklessly to make either orally or in writing to the auditors any statement which is misleading, false or deceptive in any particular material.

The auditors' report is to be read before the company in general meeting and must be open to inspection by any member.

The auditors' report must state the names of the auditors and be signed by them.

Legal position of Auditors

An auditor is not an officer of the company. He is, however, a servant of the company and for certain purposes he is an agent of the company.

Meetings

Auditors may attend general meetings of the company. They must be sent notices and communications relating to general meetings. They may speak at any general meeting on any matter which concerns them as auditors.

Duties of an Auditor

(a) He must act honestly and with reasonable skill and care.
(b) He must ascertain the true financial position of the company as shown by the books of accounts.
(c) He must verify the existence of the company's securities.
(d) He must check the cash in hand and the bank balance.
(e) He must check that borrowing is authorized and is in accordance with the articles.
(f) He must see that payments have been authorized.

In *Re Republic of Bolivia Exploration Syndicate Ltd.* [1914] 1 Ch 139 it was said that auditors "are bound to know or make themselves acquainted with their duties under the articles of the company whose accounts they are appointed to audit and under the Companies Act for the time being in force".

In *Re Kingston Cotton Mill Co.* (No.2) [1896] 2 Ch 279, the duty of an auditor in the performance of his duties was stated as follows:

> "It is the duty of an auditor to bring to bear on the work he has to perform that skill, care, and caution which a reasonably competent, careful and cautious auditor would use. . . He is a watch-dog but not a bloodhound."

In *Fomento (Sterling Area) Ltd.* v *Selsdon Fountain Pen Co. Ltd.* [1958], Lord Denning said:

> "An auditor is not to be confined to the mechanics of checking vouchers and making mathematical computations. . .His vital task is to take care to see that errors are not made, be the errors of computation or errors of omission or commission or downright untruths".

Liability in Negligence

An auditor is liable to the company in negligence for loss occasioned by breach of his duty to take care. The company must, however, prove that the auditor failed to perform his duty with reasonable care and skill.

In *Leeds Estate Building and Investment Co.* v *Shepherd* [1889], the auditor failed to check the articles of the company which provided that directors' remuneration should only be paid in certain circumstances. Remuneration was paid outside the provision. It was held that the auditor was personally liable for the payment.

The auditors may be liable to third parties in negligence if they give advice or information without taking reasonable care *(Hedley Byrne and Co. Ltd.* v *Heller and Partners Ltd.* [1964]). Under the *Hedley Byrne* case auditors may also have a duty of care to potential shareholders who may have relied on their audit and report to invest in the company.

CHAPTER 19

Accounts and Audit

Accounts

A detailed examination of the form and contents of the accounts of a company registered in the Region is outside the scope of this work. Some of the legal requirements relating to accounts of the company in the Region are, however, considered.

The main purpose of the legal requirements is essentially to protect the interests of shareholders and creditors and those who manage the company. Increasingly, however, the accounts of a company have acquired value for those contemplating investing in the company and for employees of the company for the purpose of bargaining for improved terms and conditions of employment.

Up to the end of the 19th century, legal requirements as to the accounts to be kept and as to disclosure of the company's affairs were minimal, the view being that record-keeping and financial statements were private or domestic matters for the company and its shareholders. (This can be seen from the Belize and Guyana provisions which were based on the United Kingdom Act of 1908.)

The 1929 Companies Act of the U.K. made provisions for the publication of a profit and loss account and a balance sheet with a director's report which are to be laid before the company in a general meeting. Certain details are to be stated in the balance sheet. This can be seen in the Trinidad and Tobago Companies Act (Ch 31 No. 1) which was based on the 1929 Act of the U.K.

The U.K. Act of 1948 extended the provisions concerning disclosure of information by increasing the details to be found in the profit and loss account and the balance sheet and provided for any member or debenture-holder of a public company to be entitled to a copy of the last balance sheet and the auditors report. (This can be seen from the provisions in the Jamaica Companies Act.)

The legislative trend over the years has been to impose higher standards and increase the disclosure of financial conditions and to systematize the forms and contents in which financial information may be presented both to shareholders and the public. Under the Barbados Companies Act 1982, the Bahamas Companies Act 1992 and the Guyana Companies Act 1991, for example, provisions are made for copies of the financial statements of companies to be sent to the Registrar of Companies for filing.

Except for the very recent legislation of Barbados, the Bahamas and Guyana, most of the territories in the Region have failed to update their legislative provisions to keep in step with modern trends. In practice, however, companies have followed modern accounting procedures and practice in preparing their accounts.

Modern Accounting Practice

Modern accounting practice has, in fact, outstripped the legal requirements in the Region. The accounting bodies in the Region have tried to bridge the gap by adopting accounting standards for their profession. The accounting standards adopted are a mixture of British, international and locally generated standards, creating uniformity of reporting and disclosure requirements in the financial statements throughout the Region.

The modern practices of the accounting bodies in no way supersede the legislative provisions. They merely supplement those provisions in order to observe professional standards recognized internationally[1].

Legislative Financial Provisions for Individual Territories in the Region

● BELIZE – Chapter 206, Companies Act 1914

(1) Keeping of Accounts
There are no substantive provisions in the Act dealing with the keeping of accounts by a company.

It is Table A of the First Schedule, Articles 103 to 108, that deals with this matter. It is to be remembered that it is not compulsory that these Articles be part of the Articles of a company limited by shares as they may be omitted.

Articles 103 - 108 provide for the following:

(a) the directors must keep true accounts:

   (i) of the sums of money received and expended by the company and the matter in respect of which the receipt and expenditure took place;

   (ii) of the assets and liabilities of the company;

(b) the books of account are to be kept at the registered office of the company or such other place as the directors think fit;

(c) the books of account are always to be opened to the inspection of *directors*;

(d) the directors are to determine whether and to what extent the accounts and the books of the company are to be opened to the inspection of the members;

(e) once in every year the directors are to lay before the company in general meeting a profit and loss account and a balance sheet for the current period made up to a date not more than six months before the meeting;

(f) the balance sheet is to be accompanied by a report of the directors as to:

   (i) the state of the company's affairs;

   (ii) any dividend recommended; and

   (iii)any amount to be transferred to a reserve fund.

(g) a copy of the balance sheet and the directors' report are to be sent to the persons entitled to receive notices of general meetings seven days before the meeting.

(2) Accounts and Balance Sheets
Sections 111 and 112 of the Belize Companies Act provide for the appointment of auditors and for their powers and duties.

It is a duty of the auditors to make a report to the shareholders on the accounts examined by them and on the balance sheet laid before the company in general meeting.

The auditors' report must state:

(a)   whether or not the auditors have obtained all the information and explanations they required;

(b)   whether in the auditors' opinion the balance sheet is properly drawn up so as to show a true and correct view of the state of the company's affairs the best of their knowledge and according to the explanation given to them and as shown by the books of the company.

The balance sheet is to be signed by two directors except where there is only one director then by that director.

(3)   The Auditors' Report

(a)   is to be attached to or be inserted at the foot of the balance sheet;

(b)   is to be read before the company in general meeting; and

(c)   is to be opened to inspection by any shareholder.

A shareholder is entitled to a copy of the balance sheet and the auditors' report on the payment of the prescribed fee.

- **Trinidad & Tobago - Companies Act 1939 (Ch 31 No 1, sections 120-128)**

(1)   Keeping of Accounts

Section 120 provides that a company is to keep proper books of account with respect to:

(a)   all sums of money received and expended by the company and the matters in respect of which the receipt and expenditure takes place;

(b)   all sales and purchases of goods by the company;

(c)   the assets and liabilities of the company.

The books of accounts are to be kept at the registered office of the company or at such other place as the directors think fit. They are to be opened at all times to the inspection of the directors. The directors are subject to penalties for failure to keep proper books of account.

(2)   Accounts and Balance Sheet

Under section 121, the directors must not, later than eighteen months after incorporation of the company and subsequently, once in every calendar year, lay before the company in general meeting a profit and loss account or in the case of a company not trading for profit, an income and expenditure account, for the period since incorporation in the first instance or since the preceding account.

The directors must also, in every calendar year, lay before the company in general meeting, a balance sheet as at the date to which the profit and loss account or the income and expenditure account is made up.

To every balance sheet there must be attached a report of the directors with respect to the state of the company's affairs, the amount recommended for payment of a dividend if any, the amount which they propose to carry to the reserve fund, general reserve or reserve account, to be shown specifically on a subsequent balance sheet. Under section 122, every balance sheet must contain a summary of the authorized share capital and the issued share capital, its liabilities and its assets and such particulars as are necessary to disclose the general nature of the liabilities and assets of the company and to distinguish between the amounts respectively of the fixed assets and the floating assets and must state how the values of the fixed assets have been arrived at.

Under separate headings, the balance sheet must show, so far as they are not written off:

(a)   preliminary expenses of the company;

(b)   any expenses incurred in connection with any issue of share capital or debentures;

(c)   the amount of the goodwill and any patents and trademarks as shown or otherwise ascertainable from the books.

Under section 123 assets consisting of shares in subsidiary companies is to be set out separately in the balance sheet and under section 124, the balance sheet of a holding company is to include particulars of the profits and losses of a subsidiary company.

Section 127 provides that the balance sheet must be signed on behalf of the board by two directors except where there is only one, then by that director.

It is provided in section 128 that in the case of public companies a copy of the balance sheet with documents annexed thereto and the auditor's report must be sent, not less than seven days before the general meeting, to all persons entitled to receive notices of the general meetings of the company. A member and a debenture-holder of a public company are entitled without charge to be furnished with, on demand, a copy of the last balance sheet with documents annexed thereto together with a copy of the auditor's report on the balance sheet.

Loans to directors and officers of a company must be disclosed. Remuneration of directors must also be disclosed, except that the salary of full-time directors are expressly excluded.

- **JAMAICA (Companies Act 1965, sections 142 - 155)**

(1) Keeping of Accounts

Section 142 provides that every company is to keep proper books of accounts with respect to:

(a) all sums of money received and expended by the company and the matters in respect of which the receipt and expenditure takes place;

(b) all sales and purchases of goods by the company;

(c) the assets and liabilities of the company.

The books of accounts must be kept so as to give a true and fair view of the state of the company's affairs and to explain its transactions.

The books of account are to be kept at the company's registered office or at such place as the directors think fit. They are always to be open to inspection of the directors. If the books are kept outside Jamaica, such accounts must be kept in Jamaica as will disclose with reasonable accuracy the financial position of the business at intervals not exceeding six months and which will enable the company's balance sheet and its profit and loss account to be prepared in accordance with the provisions of the Act. Failure to comply with this provision would expose the directors to penalties. The Minister has power to exempt a company from this provision.

(2) Accounts and Balance Sheet

Section 143 provides that the directors must not later than eighteen months after incorporation of the company and subsequently once in every calendar year lay before the company in general meeting, a profit and loss account (or in the case of a company not trading for profit an income and expenditure account) made up to a date not more than nine months or not more than twelve months in the case of a company having interests abroad.

The section also provides that the directors must in every calendar year cause to be made out and laid before the company in general meeting a balance sheet as at the date to which the profit and loss account (or income and expenditure account) is made up.

Attached to every balance sheet there must be a report of the directors with respect to the state of the company's affairs, the amount if any which they recommend should be paid as dividend and the amount if any which they propose to carry to the reserve fund, general reserve or reserve account shown specifically on the balance sheet or to a reserve fund, general reserve or reserve account to be shown specifically on a subsequent balance sheet. Failure to comply with these provisions render a director liable to penalties.

Section 144 provides that every balance sheet of a company must give a true and fair view of the state of affairs of the company as at the end of its financial year and every profit and loss account must give a true and fair view of the profit or loss of the company for the financial year.

The company's balance sheet and profit and loss account are to comply with the requirements of the Eighth Schedule, except so far as the requirements are modified on an application made to the Minister.

(Extract of Part I of the Eighth Schedule)

COMPANIES
EIGHTH SCHEDULE
(Section 56, 144, 147 and 375)

• ACCOUNTS

Preliminary

1 Paragraphs 2 to 11 apply to the balance sheet and 12 to 14 to the profit and loss account, and are subject to the exceptions and modifications provided for by Part II in the case of a holding company and by Part III thereof in the case of companies of the classes there mentioned; and this Schedule has effect in addition to the provisions of sections 185 and 186 of the Act.

Part I

General Provisions as to Balance Sheet and Profit and Loss Account

Balance Sheet

2 The authorized share capital, issued share capital, liabilities and assets shall be summarised, with such particulars as are necessary to disclose the general nature of the assets and liabilities, and there shall be specified:

 a any part of the issued capital that consists of redeemable preference shares, and the earliest date on which the company has power to redeem those shares;

 b so far as the information is not given in the profit and loss account, any share capital on which interest has been paid out of capital during the financial year, and the rate at which interest has been so paid;

c   the amount of the share premium account;

d   particulars of any redeemed debentures which the company has power to re-issue.

3   There shall be stated under separate headings, so far as they are not written off:

a   the preliminary expenses;

b   any expenses incurred in connection with any issue of share capital or debentures;

c   any sums paid by way of commission in respect of any shares or debentures; and

d   the amount of the discount allowed on any issue of shares at a discount.

4   (1) The reserves, provisions, liabilities and fixed and current assets shall be classified under headings appropriate to the company's business: Provided that:

a   where the amount of any class is not material, it may be included under the same heading as some other class; and

b   where any assets of one class are not separable from assets of another class, those assets may be included under the same heading.

(2) Fixed assets shall also be distinguished from current assets.

(3) The method or methods used to arrive at the amount of the fixed assets under each heading shall be stated.

5   (1) The method of arriving at the amount of any fixed asset shall, subject to sub-paragraph (2), be to take the difference between:

a   Its cost or, if it stands in the company's books at a valuation, the amount of the valuation; and

b   the aggregate amount provided or written off since the date or acquisition or valuation, as the case may be, for depreciation or diminutive in value,

and for the purposes of this paragraph the net amount at which any assets stand in the company's books at the appointed day (after deduction of the amounts previously provided or written off for depreciation or diminutive in value) shall, if the figures relating to the period before the appointed day cannot be obtained without of a valuation of those assets made at the appointed day and, where any of those assets made at the appointed day and, where any of those assets are sold, the said net amount less the amount of the sales shall be treated as if it were the amount of a valuation so made of the remaining assets.

(2) Sub-paragraph (1) shall not apply:

a to assets for which the figures relating to the period beginning with the appointed day cannot be obtained without unreasonable expense or delay; or

b to assets the replacement of which is provided for wholly or partly:

 i by making provision for renewals and charging the cost of replacement against the provision so made; or

 ii by charging the cost of replacement direct to revenue; or

c to any investments of which the market value (or, in the case of investments not having a market value, their value as estimated not having a market value, their value as estimated by the directors) is shown either as the amount of the investments or by way of note; or

d to goodwill, patents or trade marks.

(3) For the assets under each heading whose amount is arrived at in accordance with sub-paragraph (1) there shall be shown:

a the aggregate of the amounts referred to in paragraph (a) of that sub-paragraph; and

b the aggregate of the amounts referred to in paragraph (b) thereof.

(4) As respects the assets under each heading whose amount is not arrived at in accordance with the said sub-paragraph (1) because their replacement is provided for as mentioned in sub-paragraph (2) (b) there shall be state:

6 The aggregate amounts respectively of capital reserves, revenue reserves and provisions (other than provisions for depreciation, renewals or diminutive in value of assets) shall be stated under separate headings: Provided that:

a this paragraph shall not require a separate statement of any of the said three amounts which is not material; and

b the Minister may direct that he shall not require a separate statement of the amount of provisions where he is satisfied that that is not required in the public interest and would prejudice the company, but subject to the condition that any heading stating an amount arrived at after taking into account a provision (other than as aforesaid) shall be so framed or marked as to indicate that fact.

7 (1) There shall also be shown (unless it is shown in the profit and loss account or a statement or report annexed thereto, or the amount involved is not material):

a where the amount of the capital reserves, of the revenue reserves or of the provisions (other than provisions for depreciation, renewals or diminution in value of assets) shows an increase as compared with the amount at the end of the immediately preceding financial year, the source from which the amount of the increase has been derived; and

b where:

  i the amount of the capital reserves or of the revenue reserves shows a decrease as compared with the amount at the end of the immediately preceding financial year; or

  ii the amount at the end of the immediately preceding financial year of the provisions (other than provisions for depreciations, renewals or diminution in value of assets) exceeded the aggregate of the sums since applied and amounts still retained for the purposes thereof, the application of the amounts derived from the difference.

(2) Where the heading showing any of the reserves or provisions aforesaid is divided into sub-heading, this paragraph shall apply to each of the separate amounts shown in the sub-headings instead of applying to the aggregate amount thereof.

8 (1) There shall be shown under separate headings:

a the aggregate amounts respectively of the company's trade investments, quoted investments other than trade investments and unquoted investments other than trade investments;

b if the amount of the goodwill and of any patents and trade marks or part of that amount is shown as a separate item in or is otherwise ascertainable from the books of the company, or from any contract for the sale or purchase of any property to be acquired by the company, or from any documents in the possession of the company relating to the stamp duty payable in respect of any such company relating to the stamp duty payable in respect of any such contract or the conveyance of any such property, the said amount so shown or ascertained so far as not written off or, as the case may be, the said amount so far as it is shown or ascertainable and as so shown or ascertained, as the case may be;

c the aggregate amount of any outstanding loans made under the authority of provisos (b) and (c) of subsection (1) of section 54 of the Act;

d the aggregate amount of bank loans and overdrafts;

e   the net aggregate amount (after deduction of income tax) which is recommended for distribution by way of dividend.

(2) Nothing in head (b) of sub-paragraph (1) shall be taken as requiring the amount of the goodwill, patents and trade marks to be stated otherwise than as a single item.

(3) The heading showing the amount of the quoted investments other than trade investments shall be subdivided, where necessary, to distinguish the investments as respects which there has, and those as respects which there has not, been granted a quotation or permission to deal on a recognized stock exchange.

9   Where any liability of the company is secured otherwise than by operation of law on any assets of the company, the fact that liability is so secured shall be stated, but it shall not be necessary to specify the assets on which the liability is secured.

10   Where any of the company's debentures are held by a nominee of or trustee for the company, the nominal amount of the debentures and the amount at which they are stated in the books of the company shall be stated.

11   (1) The matters referred to in sub-paragraphs (2) to (11) inclusive shall be stated by way of note, or in a statement or report annexed, if not otherwise shown.

(2) The number, description and amount of any shares in the company which any person has an option to subscribe for, together with the following particulars of the option, that is to say:

a   the period during which it is exercisable;

b   the price to be paid for shares subscribed for under it.

(3) The amount of any arrears of fixed cumulative dividends on the company's shares and the period for which the dividends or, it there is more than one class, each class of them are in arrear, the amount to be stated before deduction of income tax, except that, in the case of tax free dividends, the amount shall be shown free of tax and the fact that it is so shown also be stated.

(4) Particulars of any charge on the assets of the company to secure the liabilities of any other person, including, where practicable, the amount secured.

(5) The general nature of any other contingent liabilities not provided for and, where practicable, the aggregate amount or estimated amount of those liabilities, if it is material.

(6) Where practicable the aggregate amount or estimated amount, if it is material, of contracts for capital expenditure, so far as not provided for.

(7) If in the opinion of the directors any of the current assets have not a

value, on realisation in the ordinary course of the company's business, at least equal to the amount at which they are stated, the fact that the directors are of that opinion.

(8) The aggregate market value of the company's quoted investments, other than trade investments, where it differs from the amount of the investment as stated, and the stock exchange value of any investments of which the market value is shown (whether separately or not) and is taken as being higher than their stock exchange value.

(9) The basis on which foreign currencies have been converted into sterling, where the amount of the assets or liabilities affected is material.

(10) The basis on which the amount, if any, set aside for income tax is computed.

(11) Except in the case of the first balance sheet laid before the company after the appointed day, the corresponding amounts at the end of the immediately preceding financial year for all items shown in the balance sheet.

Profit and Loss Account

12   (1) There shall be shown:

a   the amount charged to revenue by way of provision for depreciation, renewals or diminution in value of fixed assets;

b   the amount of the interest on the company's debentures and other fixed loans:

c   the amount of the charge for income tax and other taxation on profits, including, where practicable, any taxation imposed elsewhere to the extent of the relief, if any, from income tax and distinguishing where practicable between income tax and other taxation;

d   the amounts respectively provided for redemption of share capital and for redemption of loans;

e   the amount, if material, set aside or proposed to be set aside to, or withdrawn from, reserves;

f   subject to sub-paragraph (2) the amount, if material, set aside to provisions other than provisions for depreciation, renewals or dinimution in value of assets or, as the case may be, the amount, if material, withdrawn such other provisions and not applied for the purposes thereof;

g   the amount of income from investments, distinguishing between trade investments and other investments;

h   the aggregate amount of the dividends paid and proposed.

(2) the Minister may direct that a company shall not be obliged to show an amount set aside to provisions in accordance with sub-paragraph (1) (f) if he is satisfied that that is not required in the public interest and would prejudice the company, but subject to the condition that any heading stating an amount arrived at after taking into account the amount set aside as aforesaid shall be so framed or marked as to indicate that fact.

13   If the remuneration of the auditors is not fixed by the company in general meeting, the amount thereof shall be shown under a separate heading, and for the purposes of this paragraph, any sums paid by the company in respect of the auditors' expenses shall be deemed to be included in the expression "remuneration".

14   (1) The matters referred to in sub-paragraphs (2) to (6) inclusive shall be stated by way of note, if not otherwise shown.

(2) If depreciation or replacement of fixed assets is provided for by some method other than depreciation charge or provision for renewals, or is not provided for, the method by which it is provided for or the fact that it is not provided for, as the case may be.

(3) The basis on which the charge for income tax is computed.

(4) Whether or not the amount stated for dividends paid and proposed is for dividends subject to deduction of income tax.

(5) Except in the case of the first profit and loss account laid before the company after the appointed day the corresponding amounts for the immediately preceding financial year for all items shown in the profit and loss account.

(6) Any material respects in which any items shown in the profit and loss account are affected:

a   by transaction of a sort not usually undertaken by the company or otherwise by circumstances of an exceptional or non-recurrent nature; or

b   by any change in the basis of accounting.

Section 150 provides that every balance sheet of a company must be signed on behalf of the company by two directors except where there is only one director, then by that director.

Section 151 provides that a copy of every balance sheet including every document required by law to be annexed thereto, which is to be laid before the company in general meeting together with an auditors report, must, not less than twenty-one days before the date of the meeting, be sent to every member of the company (whether he is or is not entitled to receive notice of general meetings of the company), every holder of debentures of the company (whether he is or is not so entitled) and all other persons who are so entitled.

Any member or debenture holder of a public company is entitled to be furnished on demand without charge with a copy of the last balance sheet and any document annexed thereto, together with a copy of the auditors' report on the balance sheet - (sub 2).

A member or debenture holder of a private company is entitled within ten days' request to be supplied with a copy of the balance sheet and auditor's report on the payment of a fee not exceeding five cents for every hundred words.

Obligations to lay Group Accounts before Holding Company

Section 145 provides that where at the end of its financial year a company has subsidiaries, group accounts dealing with the state of affairs, and profit or loss of the company and the subsidiaries, these should be laid before the company in general meeting when its own balance sheet and profit and loss account are being laid.

Group accounts are not required:
(a)   where the company is the wholly owned subsidiary of another company incorporated in Jamaica;
(b)   the directors are of the opinion that:
    (i)   it is impracticable or would be of no real value to the members in view of the insignificant amounts involved or would involve expense or delay out of all proportion to the value to the members; or
    (ii)   the result would be misleading or harmful to the business of the company or any of its subsidiaries; or
    (iii)   the business of the holding company and that of the subsidiary are so different that they cannot reasonably be treated as a single undertaking.

In the case of (iii) and in the case when they are said to be harmful to the business, group accounts can only be dispensed with by the approval of the Minister.

For the purposes of section 145, a company is the wholly owned subsidiary of another if it has no members except that other and that other's wholly owned subsidiaries and its or their nominees - (s. 145 (4)).

The group accounts usually comprise a consolidated balance sheet and a consolidated profit and loss account of the company and its subsidiaries. Group accounts may be wholly or partly incorporated in the company's own balance sheet and profit and loss account.

Group accounts must give a true and fair view of the state of affairs and profit and loss of the company and the subsidiaries dealt with thereby as a whole, so far as concerns members of the company.

The group accounts if prepared as consolidated accounts must comply with the requirements of the Eighth Schedule so far as applicable thereto and if not so prepared must give the same or equivalent information.

The Minister may, on application or with the consent of the directors, modify the requirements for the purpose of adapting them to the circumstances of the company.

The directors of a holding company should secure except where in their opinion there are good reasons against it, that the financial year of each of its subsidiaries coincides with the company's own financial year.

(Part II of the Eighth Schedule)

COMPANIES

Part II

Special Provisions where the Company is a Holding or Subsidiary company

Modifications of and Additions to Requirements as to Company's own Accounts

15 (1) This paragraph shall apply where the company is a holding company, whether or not it is itself a subsidiary of another body corporate.
(2) The aggregate amount of assets consisting of shares in, or amounts owing (whether on account of a loan or otherwise) from the company's

subsidiaries, distinguishing shares from indebtedness, shall be set out in the balance sheet separately from all the other assets of the company, and the aggregate amount of indebtedness (whether on account of a loan or otherwise) to the company's subsidiaries shall be so set out separately from all its other liabilities and:

a   the references in Part I to the company's investments shall not include investments in its subsidiaries required by this paragraph to be separately set out; and

b   paragraph 5, sub-paragraph (1) (a) of paragraph 12 and sub-paragraph (2) of paragraph 14 shall not apply in relation to fixed assets consisting of interests in the company's subsidiaries.

(3) There shall be shown by way of note on the balance sheet or in a statement or report annexed thereto the number, description and amount of the shares in and debentures of the company held by its subsidiaries of their nominees, but excluding any of these shares or debentures in the case of which the subsidiary is concerned as personal representative in the case of which it is concerned as trustee and neither the company nor any subsidiary thereof is beneficially interested under the trust, otherwise than by way of security only for the purposes of a transaction entered into by it in the ordinary course of a business which includes the lending of money.

(4) Where group accounts are not submitted, there shall be annexed to the balance sheet a statement showing:

a   the reasons why subsidiaries are not dealt with in group accounts;

b   the net aggregate amount so far as it concerns members of the holding company and is not dealt with in the company's accounts of the subsidiaries' profits after deducting the subsidiaries' losses (or vice versa):

     i   for the respective financial years of the subsidiaries ending with or during the financial year of the company; and

     ii   for their previous financial years since they respectively became the holding company's subsidiary;

c   the net aggregate amount of the subsidiaries' profits after deducting the subsidiaries' losses (or vice versa):

     i   for the respective financial years of the subsidiaries ending with or during the financial year of the company; and

     ii   for their other financial years since they respectively became the holding company's subsidiary,

     so far as those profits are dealt with, or provisions made for those losses, in the company's accounts;

d   any qualifications contained in the report of the auditors of the subsidiaries on their accounts for their respective financial years ending as aforesaid, and any note or saving contained in those accounts to call attention to the matter which, apart from the note or saving, would properly have been referred to in such a qualification, in so far as the matter which is the subject of the qualification or note is not covered by the company's own accounts and is material from the point of view of its members.

or, in so far as the information required by this sub-paragraph is not obtainable, a statement that it is not obtainable:

Provided that the Minister may, on the application or with the consent of the company's directors, direct that in relation to any subsidiary this sub-paragraph shall not apply or shall apply only to such extent as may be provided be provided by the direction.

(5) Paragraphs (b) and (c) of sub-paragraph (4) shall apply only to profits and losses of the subsidiary which may properly be treated in the holding company's accounts as revenue profits or losses, and the profits and losses attributable to any shares in a subsidiary for the time being held by the holding company or any other of its subsidiaries shall not (for that or any other purpose) be treated as aforesaid so far as they are profits or losses for the period before the date on or as from which the shares were acquired by the company or any of its subsidiaries, except that they may in a proper case be so treated where:

a   the company is itself the subsidiary of another body corporate; and

b   the shares where acquired from that body corporate or a subsidiary of it,

and for the purpose of determining whether any profits or losses are to be treated as profits or losses for the said period the before the date on or as from which the the shares were acquired by the company or any of its subsidiaries, except that they may in a proper case be so treated where:

a   the company is itself the subsidiary of another body corporate; and

b   the shares were acquired from that body corporate or a subsidiary of it, and for the purpose of determining whether any profits or losses are to be treated as profits or losses for the said period the profit or loss for any financial year of the subsidiary may, if it is not practicable to apportion it with reasonable accuracy by reference to the facts, be treated as accruing from day to day during that year and be apportioned accordingly.

(6) Where group accounts are not submitted, there shall be annexed to the balance sheet a statement showing in relation to the subsidiaries (if any) whose financial years did not end with that of the company:

a   the reasons why the company's directors consider that the subsidiaries' financial years should not end with that of the company; and

b   the dates on which the subsidiaries' financial years ending last before that of the company respectively ended or the earliest and latest of those dates.

16   (1) The balance sheet of a company which is a subsidiary of another body corporate, whether or not it is itself a holding company, shall show the aggregate amount of its indebtedness to all bodies corporate of which it is subsidiary or a fellow subsidiary and the aggregate amount of the indebtedness of all such bodies corporate to it, distinguishing in each case between indebtedness in respect of debentures and otherwise.
(2) For the purpose of this paragraph, a company shall be deemed to be a fellow subsidiary or the same body corporate but neither is the other's.

Consolidated Accounts of Holding Company and Subsidiaries

17   Subject to the following paragraphs of this part the consolidated balance sheet and profit and loss account shall combine the information contained in the separate balance sheets and profit and loss accounts of the holding company and of the subsidiaries dealt with by the consolidated accounts, but with such adjustments (if any) as the directors of the holding company think necessary.

18   Subject as aforesaid and to Part III the consolidated accounts shall, in giving the said information, comply, so far, as practicable, with the requirements of the Act as if they were the accounts of an actual company.

19   Sections 185 and 186 of the Act shall not, by virtue of paragraphs 17 and 18, apply for the purpose of the consolidated accounts.

20   Paragraph 7 shall not apply for the purpose of any consolidated accounts laid before a company with the first balance sheet so laid after the appointed day.

21   In relation to any subsidiaries of the holding company not dealt with by the consolidated accounts:

a   sub-paragraphs (2) and (3) of paragraph 15 shall apply for the purpose of those accounts as if those accounts were the accounts of an actual company of which they were subsidiaries; and

b   there shall be annexed the like statement as is required by

> sub-paragraph (4) of that paragraph where there are no group accounts, but as if references therein to the holding company's accounts were references to the consolidated accounts.

22   In relation to any subsidiaries (whether or not dealt with by the consolidated accounts), whose financial years did not end with that of the company there shall be annexed the like statement as is required by sub-paragraph (6) of paragraph 15 where there are no group accounts.

Other Requirements as to Accounts

There must be shown in the accounts of a company laid before the general meeting:

(a)   the aggregate amount of the director's emoluments;

(b)   the aggregate amount of directors or past directors' pensions;

(c)   the aggregate amount of any compensation to directors or past directors in respect of loss of office. (See Section 185)

(d)   the amount of any loans made during the company's financial year to: (Section 186)

  (i)   any officer of the company; or

  (ii)   any person who, after the making of the loan, becomes during that year an officer of the company and made guarantee or secured by the company or a subsidiary thereof.

SPECIMEN OF AN ANNUAL REPORT

_____ LIMITED 199   ANNUAL REPORT

DIRECTOR'S REPORT

The Directors are pleased to present their report and the audited statement of accounts for the year ended 31st December, 199 .

I   **Financial Statements**   19
                                  $'000

Group profit before tax
Less provision for taxation
Group profit after tax
Balance January I
Proposed dividend
        Interim
        Final
Balance at
31 December 199
Earnings Per Share

2   **Dividends**

Your directors approved payment of an interim dividend of 10 cents per share to members on register on 1st April 199   and, in addition, they recommend the payment of a final dividend of 14 cents per share for members on register on 1st July, 199 .

3   **Directors**

In accordance with Article 95 of the Articles of Association:
Messrs   and   appointed by the Board on 15th February, 199 offer themselves for re-election.

    Mr   resigned from the Board on 15th February, 199 , on his being transferred back to the UB Group.

    In accordance with Article 89 of the Articles of Association,
Messrs   and   retire by rotation and being eligible offer themselves for re-election.

4   **Auditors**

The auditors Messrs   have signified their willingness to continue in office.

BY ORDER OF THE BOARD

_____

SECRETARY

LIMITED 199   ANNUAL REPORT

AUDITORS' REPORT

To the members of

_____

We have examined the financial statements set out on Statements II to VI and have obtained all the information and explanations which we required. Our examination was made in accordance with generally accepted auditing standards and accordingly included such tests of the accounting records and such other auditing procedures as we considered necessary.

In our opinion, proper accounting records have been kept and the financial statements, which are in agreement therewith, give a true and fair view of the state of affairs of the group and the company at December 31, 199 and of the net profit of the group and the company and the cash flows of the group for the year then ended, so far as concerns members of the company, and comply with the provisions of the Companies Act.

_____

Chartered Accountants

LIMITED 199   ANNUAL REPORT

CONSOLIDATED BALANCE SHEET AT DECEMBER 31, 199

		Statement II	
		199	199
Notes	$'000	$'000	$'000

CURRENT ASSETS

Cash and bank balances
Accounts receivable and
    prepayments
Inventories
Income tax recoverable
Due from associated company

CURRENT LIABILITIES

Bank overdraft
Income tax payable
Accounts payable and accruals
Dividend payable
Proposed dividends
Due to holding company
Due to fellow subsidiary
    companies

NET CURRENT ASSETS

INVESTMENTS

LONG-TERM RECEIVABLE

FIXED ASSETS

SHAREHOLDERS' EQUITY

Share capital
Share premium
Capital reserve
Revenue reserve
Profit and loss account

_____)
_____) Directors

The notes on Statement VI form an integral part of the financial statements.
(Notes are omitted.)

LIMITED 199   ANNUAL REPORT

CONSOLIDATED PROFIT AND LOSS ACCOUNT
YEAR ENDED DECEMBER 31, 199

Statement III

	Notes	199 $'000	199 $'000

Sales
Less discounts and rebates
Net sales
Cost of sales
Gross profit
Less expenses
Trading profit (loss)
Less interest

PROFIT (LOSS) BEFORE TAX

Share of profit of Associated Company
(199 - 15 months;
199 - 12 months)

PROFIT (LOSS) AFTER TAX

Balance, January 1
Proposed dividends

BALANCE, DECEMBER 31

Retained in the accounts of:
  The company
  Subsidiary company
  Associated company

Earnings (loss) per share

_____)
_____) Directors

The notes on Statement VI form an integral part of the financial statements.
(Notes are omitted.)

LIMITED 199   ANNUAL REPORT

BALANCE SHEET AT DECEMBER 31, 199

		Statement IV	
		199	199
	Notes	$'000	$'000	$'000

CURRENT ASSETS
Cash and bank balances
Accounts receivable and
   prepayments
Inventories
Income tax recoverable
Due from associated
   company

CURRENT LIABILITIES
Bank overdraft
Income tax payable
Accounts payable and accruals
Dividend payable
Proposed dividends
Due to holding company
Due to fellow subsidiary
   companies

NET CURRENT ASSETS
INVESTMENTS
LONG TERM RECEIVABLE
FIXED ASSETS
SHAREHOLDERS' EQUITY
Share capital
Share premium
Capital reserve
Revenue reserve
   Profit and loss account

_____)
_____) Directors

The notes on Statement VI form an integral part of the financial statements.
(Notes are omitted.)

- **BARBADOS – Companies Act 1982 (Sections 172 - 173)**

(1) **Keeping of Accounts**

Sections 172 and 173 provide that a company is to prepare and maintain adequate accounting records to be kept at the registered office of the company or at some other place in Barbados designated by the directors. Such records are to be available for inspection by the directors at all reasonable times.

If the accounting records are to be kept at a place outside Barbados, then accounting records that are adequate to enable the directors to ascertain the financial position of the company with reasonable accuracy on a quarterly basis must be kept at the registered office or other place designated by the directors.

(2) **Annual Financial Returns**

Under section 147 the directors of a company must place before the shareholders at every annual meeting of the shareholders of the company:

(a) Comparative financial statements as prescribed relating to:
  (i) the twelve months from the date the company came into existence and each subsequent financial year;
(b) report of the auditors (if any);
(c) any further information respecting the financial position of the company and the results of this operation by the articles, its by-laws or any unanimous shareholder agreement.

Exception may be given by the Registrar under section 148.

Section 150 provides that the financial statements must be approved by the directors. Approval is evidenced by the signature of one or more directors.

Section 151 provides that not less than twenty-one days before each annual meeting of the shareholders or before the signing or a resolution in lieu of the annual meeting, the company must send a copy of the financial statements to each shareholder, except a shareholder who has informed the company in writing that he does not want a copy.

Under section 152 a company:

(a) that is a public company; or
(b) that has gross revenues in its most recent financial statements exceeding $250,000 or has assets exceeding one million dollars must, unless exempted by the Registrar under subsection (3) of the section, send a copy of the financial documents to the Registrar not less than twenty-one days before each annual

meeting of the shareholders or forthwith after the signing of a resolution in lieu of an annual meeting.

Any interim financial statements sent to shareholders must also be filed forthwith with the Registrar.

The financial statements and auditors' report are, except as otherwise provided, to be prepared in accordance with standards approved by the Institute of Chartered Accountants of Barbados.

• THE BAHAMAS – Companies Act 1992 (18 of 1992)

(Came into effect on 1 August 1992)

(1) **Keeping of Accounts**

Under this heading, the Bahamas has similar provisions as Belize. See Articles 99 - 104 of the First Schedule of the Act.

(2) **Financial Disclosures (sections 123 - 129)**

The provisions dealing with financial disclosures are a shortened version of the Barbados provisions. These provisions do not apply to private companies.

Section 123 provides that the directors are to place before the members at every annual general meeting of the company:

(a)   comparative financial statements in the approved form;

(b)   the report of the auditors;

(c)   any further information respecting the financial position of the company and the results of its operations required by the articles or any unanimous shareholder agreement.

Under section 127 not less than twenty-one days before each general meeting, the company must send a copy of the annual financial statement to each member unless waived by a member.

Section 128 provides that the Registrar may, at any time, in writing, request from the company a copy of the annual financial statement and the request is to be complied with within two days after the receipt of the request.

Under section 134 auditors are required to make a report to the members on the accounts examined by them and on every balance sheet laid before the company in general meeting. The auditors in their report must state whether in their opinion, the balance sheet was drawn up in accordance with the national accounting standards approved by a recognized professional body of chartered accountants in the Bahamas, so as to give a fair representation of the company's affairs.

- **GUYANA**

(1)   **Existing Provisions**
Cap 80:01, s 122
Articles 103 - 108, Table A
Under the existing law of Guyana, provisions are similar to the Belize
provisions which are based on 1908 Act of the U.K.

(2)   **Companies Act 1991 (29 of 1991)[2]**
N.B. This Act at the time of going to press has not been brought into
force by virtue of section 1.
Sections 152 to 186 deal with financial disclosures including the keeping
of accounts and the powers and duties of auditors.
  Provisions are similar to the provisions of Jamaica with some variation.

- **ST KITTS, NEVIS, ANGUILLA AND ST VINCENT**

The Companies Acts of these territories were based on the 1862 Act of
the U.K.
  There is a requirement that the directors "cause true accounts to be
kept of the stock-in-trade of the company; of the sums of money
received and expended by the company, and the matter in respect of
which such receipts and expenditure take place; and of the credits and
liabilities of the company".
  The directors have to present a balance sheet accompanied by a
statement of income and expenditure to the members once a year
showing a just balance of profit or loss. Guidance on the contents and
format of the balance sheet and how the profit or loss is to be arrived at
is given. The balance sheet must contain a summary of the assets and
liabilities of the company and the statement of income and expenditure
should show:
(a)   the amount of gross income distinguishing the several sources
      from which it has been derived;
(b)   the amount of gross expenditure distinguishing the expense of
      the establishment, salaries and other like matters;
(c)   every item of expenditure fairly chargeable against the year's
      income; and
(d)   in cases where any item of expenditure, which may in fairness be
      distributed over several years, has been incurred in any one year,
      the whole amount of such item shall be stated, with the addition
      of the reasons why only a portion of such expenditure is
      charged against the income of the year.

Notes

1. See Margaret Mendes, *The Regulatory Framework of Accounting in the Caribbean* (CFM Publications, 1987).
2. This Act at the time of going to press has not been brought into force by virtue of section 1.

CHAPTER 20

Reconstruction, Mergers, Take-overs and Arrangements

Sometimes a company may wish to reorganize itself without involving outsiders. It may do this:

(a) by forming a new company and transferring its assets to the new company, the members of the new company remaining substantially the same; this is usually referred to as a reconstruction; or

(b) by entering into a scheme of arrangement or compromise with its creditors and/or members, particularly, if it is in the process of being wound up.

A company may also join with another company under the name of one of these companies or under the name of a new company which was formed for this purpose. This is commonly referred to as a merger or an amalgamation. (The two terms are used interchangeably.)

Sometimes a company may acquire sufficient shares in another company to enable it to exercise control over the other company (the "target" company). The target company will remain in existence but as a subsidiary of the controlling company. When this occurs, it is referred to as a take-over.

A take-over is different from a merger in the sense that in a take-over both companies remain in existence for the time being. In a merger one or both of the companies will go out of existence.

The legislation in the Region contains few provisions which have direct application to mergers and take-overs probably because of the low levels of economic performance and limited resources. It is, however, common to find some provisions dealing with reconstructions and arrangements, especially on a winding-up.

Provisions are normally found which allow a company liable to be wound-up to enter into an arrangement or compromise with its creditors and/or members or any class of them. These provisions may be used to effect a merger. The procedure to be followed usually requires the approval of the court, the aim being to safeguard the position of the minority shareholders and outsiders.

Reconstruction and Mergers

There are various methods in which a reconstruction or a merger can be accomplished.

A company's objects clause in the memorandum of association generally gives the company an express power to sell its undertaking and property to another company in return for shares in that other company. If this power is exercised, the old company would be wound up, and its members would become members in the new company. It is common to find that such a sale must be authorized by special resolution. It is also common in the Region for the legislation to provide that where a company is proposed to be or is being wound up, the liquidator has power to sell, with the sanction of a special resolution of the company, the undertaking or property of the company for shares in another company and the members would become shareholders in the other company. Any such sale is binding on the members of the transferor company but dissentients shares are to be bought out. (See, for example, the Companies Acts for Belize, s 183; Guyana (Cap 89:01) s 196; Jamaica s 264; Trinidad and Tobago, s 222.)

Compromises and Arrangements

A Company has an implied power to compromise disputes in which it is involved with outsiders or with its own members. In any event an express power is usually given in the objects clause of its memorandum allowing for this.

The Region's legislation[1] normally provide a machinery to be followed where a compromise or arrangement is being effected on the part of a company. The aim is to protect the rights of others that may be adversely affected.

Procedure for Compromises and Arrangements

(1) The company, or any creditor or member or liquidator, if the company is being wound up, may apply to the Court to order meetings of the creditors or a class of the creditors and of the members or a class of the members;

(2) The company must in each case send out the notice calling a meeting and a statement explaining any material interests of the directors and its effect.

(3) The compromise or arrangement must be agreed at each meeting held by a majority representing seventy-five percent in value of those voting in person or by proxy;

(4) After the meetings are held, the court must give its approval to compromise;

(5) Copy of the order of the court must be delivered to the Registrar of Companies for registration and a copy must be annexed to the memorandum of association issued after the order was made.

Note

1. See the Companies Acts for:
    Belize (Cap. 206) s 119
    Guyana (Cap. 89:01) s 128
    Jamaica ss 192 - 195
    Barbados ss 206, 223, 224

CHAPTER 21

Insider Dealing or Trading

The term "insider dealing" or "insider trading" is generally used to mean the dealing in the securities of a company by a person who has inside information about them which has a substantial bearing on the value of those securities. The insider is usually in close proximity to the company, e.g. as a director or other officer of the company with easy access to confidential information.

Insider trading takes many forms. A common example is where there is a take-over bid for the shares of a company and a profitable offer is being made to the directors in confidence. The directors armed with this information may buy up for themselves the shares of unsuspecting shareholders and then sell them at a great profit when the take-over takes place.

Again, directors and other insiders who have confidential knowledge of the rapidly declining state of the company's business may dispose of their shares in the company in time to avoid a loss.

Until recent legislation, the only form of regulation over insider trading in the Region was the common law. Under the common law it is only in certain special cases that the law will protect the use of confidential information. There is no general principle which would deprive an insider of improper profit made through insider trading. Neither is there a general principle that the insider must make full disclosure of any inside information he may have when dealing with the other party to a transaction. For there to be a duty to disclose under the law, there must be a fiduciary relationship in existence between the parties. Where there is such a relationship, the fiduciary is not allowed to make a secret profit from his position as such.

In *Percival* v *Wright* [1902], a director purchased shares from members of the company without revealing to them that negotiations were in progress for the purchase of all the shares at a higher price. It was held that the contract between the director and those members could not be set aside as the directors as fiduciaries under a duty not to make a secret profit owed their duty to the company only and not to the members of the company. It was said that there was no duty to disclose the negotiations to the shareholders.

The temptation to indulge in insider dealings and the unfairness of such dealings are therefore obvious. Earlier legislation within the Region did not deal with insider trading. In fact it was not until the 1970s that proposals for change in the law were seriously considered in England. These proposals resulted in legislation being enacted in the United Kingdom in the form of the Companies Act 1980. In 1985 the provisions were consolidated in the Companies Securities (Insider Dealing) Act 1985.

In the recent company law legislation of Barbados, the Bahamas and Guyana there are specific provisions dealing with insider dealings which are substantially similar except that Guyana's provisions include the dealings in debentures as well as shares. In these provisions an "insider" is defined to mean:

(a) an officer of the company;

(b) a company that acquires shares issued by it or by any company in the same group of companies;

(c) a person who owns more than ten percent of the shares of a company or who exercises control or direction over more than ten percent of the votes attached to the shares in a company;

(d) a person employed or retained by a company professional technical or commercial advisers;

(e) an associate of or a company in the same group of companies as a person mentioned in paragraphs (a) to (d), above;

(f)   a company or a person who receives specific confidential information from a person described above.

The Acts provide that an insider who makes use of any specific confidential information for his own benefit or advantage, if generally known, might reasonably be expected to affect materially the value of the share (or debenture) -

(a)   is liable to compensate any person for any direct loss suffered by that person as a result of the transaction unless the information was known or could have been known in the exercise of reasonable diligence, and

(b)   is accountable to the company for any direct benefit or advantage received or receivable by the insider as a result of the transaction.

(See sections 308-311 of the Barbados Companies Act; sections 305-309 of the Guyana Companies Act, 1991; sections of the Bahamas Companies Act 1992.)

CHAPTER 22

Winding-Up

Except for Barbados[1], there are relatively few differences in principle within the Region with regard to winding-up. There is much common ground both in detail and principle, though modern statutes have, in certain respects, extended the scope of the law and have included certain requirements which are considered necessary.

Winding-up or liquidation of a company is the process by which the life of a company is brought to an end and its property distributed to its creditors and, if any remains, to the members. It is the "selling up, paying off and closing down" of the company.

The process of winding-up should be compared with placing the company in receivership[2].

Winding-up is a special area of company law. Lord Denning said of it:

> "It is one of the most difficult subjects. Both lawyers and accountants hate it. Most of them know nothing about it."

A company being an artificial entity having perpetual succession does not die like a natural person. It continues indefinitely until it is dissolved, i.e. its name removed from the register of companies by the Registrar of Companies.

A company may be dissolved without it being wound up, such as when it is transferring its undertaking to another company under a scheme for reconstruction or amalgamation. Here there is a compromise or an arrangement between the company and its creditors or members and the sanction of the court obtained. If approval is given, the company is dissolved without going through the process of winding-up.[3]

Again a company may be struck off the register of companies by the Regis,trar of Companies if the Registrar is of the opinion that the company is no longer carrying on business.

The consequence of a decision to wind up a company is broadly the appointment of a liquidator who will take control of the company for the purpose of winding-up its affairs. In this case the directors would cease to have management functions and where winding-up is by the court the employees of the company would loose their jobs.

A company can be wound up whether or not it is solvent as insolvency is not essential to start the process for winding-up.

A company may be wound up in one of three ways:

(1)   winding-up by the court – (called compulsory winding-up);
(2)   voluntary winding-up, i.e. the members pass a resolution to wind up the company;
(3)   winding-up under the supervision of the court.

This last method is voluntary winding-up with a petition for the court's supervision. This is rarely used in practice and the *CARICOM Report* recommended that it be abolished.

(1) Winding-up by the Court (Compulsory Winding Up)[4]

The court does not act on its own motion. Someone must petition the court having the necessary jurisdiction, i.e. the Supreme or High Court of the territory. This can be done by the company itself, or by a creditor or by a member (in some cases by some public officer, e.g. the official receiver). For circumstances in which a company may be compulsorily wound up by the court see, for example, section 203 of the Companies Act of Jamaica; section 197 of the Bahamas Act 1992; section 128 of Belize Companies Act Companies (Cap 206).

A company may be wound up by the Court:

(a)   if the company has by special resolution resolved that the company be wound up by the Court;
(b)   if default is made in delivering the statutory report or in holding a statutory meeting;

(c)   if the company does not commence its business within a year from its incorporation or suspends its business for a whole year;

(d)   if the number of members fall below the statutory minimum;

(e)   if the company is unable to pay its debts;

(f)   if the court is of the opinion that it is just and equitable that the company be wound up.

The most important are (e) and (f), i.e. unable to pay its debts and "just and equitable" grounds.

Unable to Pay Debts

This is the most commonly used ground. A company is unable to pay its debts if:

(a)   it is indebted in an amount exceeding a certain specified sum (e.g. in Jamaica, this is $100; in Belize $250; in the Bahamas $1,000) and a demand is made for payment and no payment is made within a specified period (3 weeks); or

(b)   execution issued on a judgement of a court in favour of a creditor is returned unsatisfied in whole or in part; or

(c)   it is proved to the satisfaction of the court, that the company is unable to pay its debts as they fall due.

Though the Court is empowered to wind up the company under this heading, it need not do this as the power is discretionary. All the circumstances will be looked at. Petition to wind up under this heading is brought by a dissatisfied creditor.

"Just and Equitable Ground"

Petition to wind up under this heading is usually brought by a member of the company. The court has held that the words "just and equitable" are of wide application and are not to be restricted.

The court under this ground has a wide discretion and can order winding-up whenever the circumstances so demand. The circumstances are difficult to define. In *Ebrahimi* v *Westbourne Galleries Ltd.* [1973], for example, the House of Lords stated that the expression is to be given its apparent broad meaning.

The court may make an order in the following cases:

(a) when the substratum of the company has gone, i.e. the main object for which the company was formed is no longer there – unusual in modern times where the objects clause is widely drawn. (See *Re German Date Coffee Co.* [1882]);

(b) where the company was formed for a fraudulent or illegal purpose;

(c) where there is a deadlock in the management of the business of the company because the directors cannot agree on vital matters and the company was formed on the basis of mutual trust and confidence and shared management similar to a partnership.

(d) where a member is unjustifiably excluded from the affairs of the company;

(e) where the directors are in control and are mismanaging the company's affairs.

In *Re Yenidje Tobacco Co. Ltd.* [1916] W and R were sole shareholders in and directors of a company with equal rights of management and voting power. After a time, they became bitterly hostile to one another and disagreed over most things. The company, however, made large profits. On a petition to wind up on the ground that it was just and equitable to do so, it was held that mutual trust and confidence had been lost and the company should be wound up.

In *Ebrahimi* v *Westbourne Galleries Ltd.* [1973] A.C. 360 (HL) from 1945 E and N were partners in a carpet dealing business, with equal share in the management and profits. In 1958, they formed a private company to take over the business. E and N were the directors. Later, N's son G was appointed director and the company made good profits. However, there was disagreement between E and N. G sided with N. At the general meeting N and G removed E as director and thereafter excluded him from the conduct of the company's business. E petitioned for winding-up on the ground that it was just and equitable. The House of Lords held that the company should be wound up as the company was formed on good faith and that E and N should manage the Company. E should not, therefore, be expelled from this. It was said that the words "just and equitable" are general words of wide application and must not be restricted. It was the "bad faith" element by the parties which made it "just and equitable" to put the company in liquidation.

In *Re A and B C Chewing Gum Limited* [1975] 1 WLR 579, the petitioners had the right to participate in management under a shareholders agreement with the company. They removed a director. The respondent directors and majority shareholders refused to recognize the removal. It was held that the company should be wound up on the ground that it was just and equitable to do so.

It is a general rule that in the case where winding-up is on the "just and equitable" ground, the petition to wind up is to be brought by a member whose shares are fully paid up. In his petition, he must show that there is a prima facie probability that the company is solvent and that there are likely to be assets available for distribution to the members. The reason is that unless there are such assets the member has no interest in a winding-up as he will get nothing.

In *Re Rica Gold Washing Co.* [1879] it was said that in petitioning for a winding-up on the "just and equitable" ground a member is not confined to such circumstances which affect him as a shareholder. He is entitled to rely on any circumstances of justice and equity which affect him in his relations with the company or with other shareholders.

Whether it is "just and equitable" to wind up a company depends on facts which exist at the time of the hearing of the petition and the petitioner is confined to the heads of complaint set out in his petition.

Consequences of a Winding-Up Order

The consequences of the making of a winding-up order by the court is that it dates back to an earlier date than that on which the order was made. This earlier date is called the commencement of the winding-up and is:

(i)   the time of the presentation of the petition; or

(ii) the time of the passing of the resolution to wind up the company, if earlier.

Provision is commonly made that any disposition of property made *by* the company after the commencement of a winding-up is void unless the court orders otherwise. The court can sanction transactions in the ordinary course of business.

Property may safely be transferred or payment made to the company during the winding up but payments made by the company must generally be refunded by the recipient.

Any transfer of shares or alteration of the status of members after the commencement date is also void.

Further, no action can proceed with or be commenced against the company except by leave of the Court.

Appointment of Liquidator

A liquidator is appointed by the court and is under the court's supervision. In the more modern legislation, creditors and members are allowed to appoint a committee of inspection which may give binding directions to the liquidator (see sections 225, 231-323 of the Jamaica Companies Act.)

Similarly the Registrar may exercise control over the liquidator and the company's officers are required to submit a statement of the affairs of the company to the Official Receiver (who is the provisional liquidator) who must report on those affairs to the court.

Committee of Inspection

After a winding-up order is made by the court, the creditors and contributories, at separate meetings, would decide whether a Committee of Inspection should be appointed to work alongside the liquidator. The Committee will comprise of both creditors and contributories agreed upon at the appropriate meetings. The committee is appointed by the court.

The appointment of a committee of inspection is a satisfactory device to ensure that the interests of creditors and contributories are taken into account by the liquidator as the committee has certain prescribed supervisory functions over the liquidator.

List of Contributories

In a compulsory winding-up, as soon as is practicable after making the winding-up order, the liquidator must settle a list of contributories, i.e. past and present members who are liable to contribute to the assets of the company on the winding-up. In the case of companies limited by shares, the liability of contributories is limited to any unpaid amount owing on their shares.

Property of the Company

When a winding-up order has been made, the liquidator must take into his custody or under his control all the property to which the company is or appears to be entitled.

Voluntary Winding-up[5]

In voluntary winding-up the decision to wind up is taken by the members in general meeting.

A company may be wound up voluntarily in the ways prescribed by legislation. These usually are:

(a) by passing an ordinary resolution when any period fixed by the articles for the duration of the company has expired or the event, if any, prescribed by the articles for its dissolution has passed;

(b) by passing a special resolution to wind up the company voluntarily;

(c) by passing an extra-ordinary resolution on the ground that the company cannot, by reason of its liabilities, continue its business.

(In earlier legislation, "c" above is not provided for.)

Kinds of Voluntary Winding-Up

In earlier legislation there is only one type of voluntary winding up. No distinction is made as in Jamaica. In Jamaica there are two types of voluntary winding-up:

1. members' voluntary winding-up;

2. creditors' voluntary winding-up.

Whether a winding-up is a *members'* or a *creditors'* voluntary winding-up will depend on whether a declaration of solvency is filed with the Registrar of Companies.

• Members' Voluntary Winding-up

A members' voluntary winding-up may only proceed as such if the majority of the directors at a board meeting make a statutory declaration to the effect that they, having made a full enquiry into the affairs of the company, have formed the opinion that the company will be able to pay its debts in full within a specified period not exceeding twelve months from the commencement of the winding up. This statutory declaration is referred to as the "declaration of solvency".

There is a duty to file the declaration of solvency with the Registrar of Companies. The declaration must be filed within five weeks immediately preceding the date of passing the resolution for winding-up. Heavy penalties are imposed for making a declaration without reasonable grounds for doing so.

A members' voluntary winding-up will therefore only take place if the company is solvent.

The resolution to wind up the company voluntarily at the general meeting will usually be a special resolution. At the said meeting a liquidator will be appointed. No creditors' meeting is held. The company being solvent all creditors will be paid off. No committee of inspection is appointed.

• Creditors' Voluntary Winding-up

If no declaration of solvency is filed with the Registrar within the period, the winding-up will proceed as a creditors' voluntary winding-up, and this is so even if the company is solvent and can pay its debts in full.

To commence a creditors' voluntary winding-up:

(a) the directors will call a general meeting of the members to pass the appropriate[1] resolution to wind up the company;

(b) the directors must also call a meeting of the creditors for the same day or the day after the general meeting;

(c) notices of the creditors' meeting must be sent to the creditors at the same time as notices of the general meeting are sent out. The notice of the creditors' meeting is advertised in the *Gazette* and a daily newspaper;

(d) the directors must lay a full statement of the company's affairs before the creditors' meeting together with a list of the creditors and the estimated amount of the claims;

(e)   the directors must appoint one of their number to preside over the creditors' meeting.

At the creditors' meeting, a person is nominated to be the liquidator. The company, at their meeting to wind up, will also appoint a liquidator. If there is a conflict in the appointments, the creditors' liquidator becomes the liquidator to wind up the company.

In a members' voluntary winding-up, if the liquidator is of the opinion that the company will not be able to pay its debts in full as the directors have stated in their statutory declaration, he is empowered to call at once a meeting of the creditors, laying before them a statement of the assets and liabilities of the company. From the date of this meeting, the winding-up becomes a creditors' voluntary winding-up.

Differences Between Members' and Creditors' Voluntary Winding-up

The main differences between a members' and creditors' voluntary winding-up are:

(a)   in a creditors' voluntary winding-up the liquidator is normally selected by creditors. In a members' voluntary winding-up, he is selected by the members;

(b)   in a creditors' voluntary winding-up there is normally a committee of inspection; this is not so in a members' voluntary winding-up.

Committee of Inspection

A committee of inspection may be appointed in a creditors' voluntary winding-up as in the case of a compulsory winding-up.

It usually comprises an equal number of representatives of members and creditors usually not more than five members from each side.

The general function of the committee is to work with the liquidator and to approve the exercise of certain of his acts and powers (as specified in the Companies Acts).

The Liquidator

On his appointment, the liquidator must, within twenty-one days after his appointment, publish in the *Gazette* and in a daily newspaper and deliver to the Registrar of Companies notice of his appointment.

The liquidator has numerous statutory powers but in the exercise of some of these powers, he must obtain the approval of the court or the committee of inspection or approval at the meetings of members or creditors.

His powers are always subject to the control of the court and any creditor or contributory may apply to the court in respect of the exercise or proposed exercise of any of these powers. The liquidator himself may always apply to the court for an order to resolve any unusual difficulty.

- **Powers of the liquidator requiring the sanction of the court or the approval of the committee of inspection**

The following are instances in which the liquidator requires the sanction of the court or the approval of the committee of inspection:

1. to conduct legal proceedings in the name of the company;
2. to carry on the business of the company as far as is necessary for the beneficial winding-up of the company;
3. to enter into compromises with creditors or contributories;
4. to pay any class of creditors in full.

- **Powers requiring no sanction**

The following can be done by the liquidator without sanctions from the court or the committee:

1. selling of the company's property;
2. drawing, accepting and indorsing bills of exchange in the company's name;
3. raising money on the security of company's assets;
4. appointing an agent;
5. appointing an attorney-at-law or a solicitor to assist him;
6. executing deeds, receipts and other documents using the seal of the company if necessary;
7. probing the bankruptcy or insolvency of a contributory;

8. doing all such other things as are necessary to wind up the company and distribute its assets.

The liquidator may summon general meetings of creditors and contributories to ascertain their wishes.

[Note the case of *Re Centrebind Ltd* [1966] where the directors convened a general meeting to wind up the company. They did not make a statutory declaration of solvency nor did they call a meeting of the creditors. A liquidator was appointed and he disposed of the assets of the company before the creditors could appoint a liquidator. It was held that the liquidator appointed by the members was validly appointed and the sale of the assets could not be challenged.]

Dissolution

When the liquidation is complete, the liquidator must, by at least one month's notice in the *Gazette*, call final meetings of the company and the creditors and present his account. Within a week after these meetings, a copy of the account and a return of the holding of the meetings must be filed with the Registrar of Companies. Three months later the company is automatically dissolved.

Consequences of a Voluntary Winding-up

The commencement date of a voluntary winding-up is the date of the passing of the resolution for voluntary winding-up.

As from the date of commencement the company must cease to carry on business, except so far as is required for its beneficial winding-up.

No transfer of shares can be made without the sanction of the liquidator and any alteration in the status of a member is void. A transfer of debentures can, however, be made.

On the appointment of a liquidator, the powers of the directors cease, except so far as the company in general meeting (or the liquidator in a members' voluntary winding-up) or the committee of inspection (or the creditors in a creditors' voluntary winding-up, if there is no such committee) sanctions their continuance.

A voluntary winding-up does not necessarily operate as a discharge of the company's employees; but if it takes place because the company is insolvent, it will operate as a discharge.

After the commencement of the winding-up the liquidator may continue the employment of the company's employees to wind up the company.

A voluntary winding-up does not bar the right of a creditor or member to have the company wound up by the court. However, the court will have regard to the wishes of all the creditors, and if the majority favour the continuance of the voluntary winding-up, an order for the company to be wound up by the court will not be made unless the petitioner can show special circumstances.

Barbados

In Barbados the provisions regarding liquidation are somewhat different than in Jamaica - (see Part IV, ss 357-385 of the Barbados Companies Act 1982).

(a) Bankrupt Company

In Barbados, if a company commits an act of bankruptcy a receiving order may be made against it under the Bankruptcy Act and if the company is adjudged bankrupt, the court may make such an order in respect of its dissolution as the court thinks fit (see sections 357-360).

(b) Shares not Issued

Under section 363 of the Act a company that has not issued shares may be dissolved at any time by resolution of all the directors.

(c) No Property or Liability

Under section 364 a company with no property and no liabilities may be dissolved by special resolution of the shareholders. If the company has issued more than one class of shares, it may be dissolved by special resolution of the holders of each class.

Where dissolution is under section 363 or 364, articles of dissolution must be sent to the Registrar and on receipt the Registrar will issue a certificate of dissolution.

Voluntary Liquidation (sections 366-367)

The directors or a shareholder who is entitled to vote at a general meeting may make a proposal for voluntary liquidation of a company and the company may be liquidated and dissolved by special resolution of the shareholders or, if the company has issued more than one class of shares, by special resolution of the holders of each class.

A statement of intent to dissolve the company must be sent to the Registrar in the prescribed form. On receipt the Registrar must issue a certificate of intent to dissolve. When the certificate is issued the company must cease to carry on business except to the extent necessary for its liquidation. Its corporate existence continues until the Registrar issues a certificate of dissolution of the company.

After a certificate of intent to dissolve is issued, the company must prepare articles of dissolution which must be sent to the Registrar who will then issue a certificate of dissolution of the company.

Dissolution by the Registrar of the Court

Under section 371, the Registrar may dissolve a company by iussuing a certificate of dissolution or he may apply to the court for an order dissolving the company, if the company:

(a) has not commenced business within three years after the date shown in its certificate of incorporation;

(b) has not carried on its business for three consecutive years;

(c) has not had its name restored to the register within two years after it was struck off by the Registrar.

Dissolution by Court

Under section 372, the Registrar or any interested person may apply to the court for an order dissolving a company, if the company:

(a) has failed for two or more consecutive years to comply with the requirements of the Act with respect to the holding of annual meetings of shareholders;

(b) has contravened certain sections of the Act as provided in section 372 (1) (b);

(c) has procured any certificate under the Act by misrepresentation.

Upon the hearing of any such application, the court may order the company to be dissolved or make such order as it thinks fit.

Under section 373, the court may order the liquidation and dissolution of a company on the application of a shareholder, on the ground that the business or affairs of the company are conducted in a manner that is oppressive or unfairly prejudicial or that it unfairly disregards the interests of any shareholder, debenture holder, creditor, director or officer of the company.

Under the section the court may also liquidate and dissolve a company on the ground that it is just and equitable for it to do so. An application under this ground must state the reasons for the liquidation and dissolution and the reasons must be verified by affidavit of the applicant.

A copy of the court's order must be published in a newspaper published or distributed in Barbados at least once in each week before the hearing and be served on the Registrar and on each person named in the order. Where a court makes an order for the liquidation of a company, then from the date stated in the order, the company is to cease to carry on business except if the business is in the opinion of the liquidator required for an orderly liquidation. The powers of the directors and shareholders will be vested in the liquidator except as specifically authorized by the court or as may be delegated by the liquidator to the directors or the shareholders - (see section 377).

The court may appoint any person, including a director, an officer or a shareholder as liquidator of the company - (section 378).

Under the Supervision of the Court

The Registrar or any interested person may, at any time during the liquidation of a company, apply to the court for an order that the liquidation be continued under the supervision of the court. The court may so order and may make any further order it thinks fit. The application must state the reasons for the application and these must be verified by the affidavit of the applicant - (see sections 368 and 374).

Notes

1. See p.227, infra.
2. See chapter 12, p.113, supra.
3. See chapter 20, p.210, supra.
4. Different provisions for Barbados (see p.227, infra).
5. For Barbados, see p.227, infra.

CHAPTER 23

External Companies

An external company is one which has been incorporated outside a territory. Under the common law, a company incorporated outside a particular territory is able to carry on business within that territory but is subject to the general law as to its capacity to sue or be sued and to own land within the territory. Such a company is normally referred to as "overseas", "foreign" or "external" company.

In any event most of the territories within the Region (though not all – e.g. St Vincent) have specific statutory provisions regulating external companies. The more modern legislation is more detailed than the older provisions.

The criterion adopted in most of the territories to determine if a company is an external company is either the establishment of a place of business within the territory or the carrying on of business within the territory.

The established practice for many companies registered outside the particular territory is to establish a place of business in the territory.

Carrying on business generally means the transaction of business regularly by the company from an office established for the purpose in the territory.

Under older legislations, a company which only employs agents within a territory but has no office has not established a place of business within the territory. (Under modern legislation this meaning has been extended to cover other situations. See, for example, the Barbados provisions at p. 234-235, *infra.)*

If a company is an external company it has to be registered as provided under the Act and must comply with the statutory provisions with regard to the filing of documents, containing vital information about the company's affairs, with the Registrar of Companies. The information filed must show:

(i)   the name of the company;
(ii)   the nature of its business;
(iii) a list of its directors;
(iv)   the names of local managers;
(v)   the company's share structure;
(vi)   the name and address of a person resident in the state authorized to accept service;
(vii) the principal office of the company in the place of incorporation;
(viii) the principal place of business in the state.

Provision is normally made that any legal process or notices may be served on an overseas company by addressing it to and leaving it or sending it by post to the person whose name has been delivered to the Registrar for this purpose.

Specific Provisions relating to certain territories

- **BELIZE (Companies Act Cap. 206 sections 248 - 249)**

In Belize, an overseas company is a company incorporated outside Belize with an established place of business in Belize.

Under section 249, within one month of the establishment of a place of business in Belize, an overseas company must deliver to the Registrar for registration the following :

(a)   a certified copy (in English) of the constitution of the company;
(b)   a list of the directors and secretary with their particulars as prescribed;
(c)   the names and addresses of some person or persons resident in Belize authorized to accept on behalf of the company service of process and notices to be served on the company.

It is also provided that any alterations must be delivered to the Registrar within twenty-one days of the alteration.

An overseas company which is registered under the Act has the power to hold lands in Belize.

In every calendar year, an overseas company must file with the Registrar a balance sheet. It must also:

(a) in every prospectus state the country in which it is incorporated;

(b) exhibit at the place where it carries on business, the name of the company and the country of incorporation;

(c) state the name of the company and the country of incorporation on every bill, letter, notices and official publication;

(d) if the liability of the members is limited this is to be stated in every prospectus, bill, letter, notices and other official publication.

There are penalties imposed on the company and its officers for failure to comply with the provisions.

- **GUYANA**

  (a) **Companies Act (Cap. 89:01 sections 259 - 261)**
  The Guyana provisions in respect of the existing law are similar to the Belize provisions except, that the filing of the particulars for registration and any alterations must be made within three months and for an external company to hold any land in Guyana it must obtain a licence from the President.

  (b) **Companies Act, (1991) (29 of 1991) [not yet in force] (sections 310 - 333)**
  Substantially similar provisions as those in the Barbados Act of 1982 (see below).

- **TRINIDAD & TOBAGO (Ch 31 No. 1, sections 297 & 307)**

The provisions are similar to the Belize provisions.

- **JAMAICA (Companies Act 1965 sections 345 - 354)**

Jamaica has the same provisions as Belize except that the time for the registration of documents with the Registrar can be extended by the Minister for up to four months.

Also, in addition to a balance sheet the company must file with the Registrar in every calendar year a profit and loss account and group accounts as necessary, as if the company was incorporated in the country – (see section 349). There are specific provisions with respect to prospectuses of external companies – (see sections 355-360 of the Act).

• BARBADOS (Companies Act 1982 sections 324 - 345)

The Barbados provisions are somewhat different and are wider in scope.

The provisions prohibit external companies from carrying on any undertaking in Barbados until registered under the Act[1].

An "external company" is any incorporated or unincorporated body formed under the laws of countries other than Barbados.

"Undertaking" is defined to include:

(a)   holding title or having interest in any land in Barbados;

(b)   maintaining an office, warehouse or place of business;

(c)   licensed or registered under any law to do business *or* to sell shares or debentures of its own.

It also provides that if an external company is listed with a telephone number in a telephone directory published in Barbados it will be presumed, unless the contrary is established, that the company is carrying on an undertaking in Barbados.

The Registrar has the power to restrict the powers and activities of an external company in certain prescribed circumstances. There is a right of appeal to the Minister.

An external company must file a statement in the prescribed form setting out particulars of itself and certain other documents as set out in section 330. The documents must be in English.

One of the documents that must be filed is a fully executed power of attorney in the prescribed form which empowers some person who is resident in Barbados to act as attorney for the company, for the purpose of accepting process against the company and also for receiving notices on its behalf.

On registration, the Registrar will issue a certificate of registration of the company.

There are similar provisions concerning the display of the name of the company at the place of business and on bills, letters and other publications as in the Belize provisions.

If an external company is not registered it cannot maintain an action or other legal proceeding in any court in Barbados in respect of any contract made in Barbados in connection with the carrying on of any undertaking by the company in Barbados. There are also provisions for the making of annual returns by external companies.

- **BAHAMAS (Companies Act 1992 sections 179 - 191)**

  (a) The Bahamas provisions are substantially similar to the Barbados provisions.

  (b) In 1990 the **International Business Companies Act** was passed to deal specifically with international business companies, i.e. companies that do not carry on business with persons resident in the Bahamas nor own any interest in real property in Bahamas other than a lease of property for use as an office nor do they carry on banking, trust, insurance business or provide a registered office for companies. Such companies must be registered as provided in the Act. However, the incorporation procedure is simpler than ordinary companies and the disclosure requirements are minimal.

Note

1. For a form of application for registration of an external company in Barbados, see Form 28 in the Third Schedule of the Companies Regulations, 1984.

CHAPTER 24

Administration and Supervision

In all member states, some machinery has been provided for supervising the affairs of a company and the operation of company law. However, the general responsibility for companies and company law is in most cases, part of the commercial portfolio of the economic or financial ministry of the territory in question, e.g. the Ministry responsible for trade or commerce.

The Registrar of Companies

All regional statutes make some provision for a Companies Registry and a Registrar of Companies. In nearly every state the functions of the Registrar are combined with other responsibilities. In most cases, the duties of the Registrar are required by law to be undertaken by the Registrar of the Supreme Court of the territory.

Jamaica, however, has an independent Registry for Companies and a Registrar who is qualified as a lawyer.

It is usually the responsibility of the Registrar to be responsible for the administration of the Companies Act.

Official Receiver

Legislation in the Region makes provisions for an Official Receiver to be appointed where there is a winding-up of the company by the Court. In some territories, the office is called "Trustee in Bankruptcy", "Official Assignee" or "Official Liquidator".

Controls over Share Trading

Stock Exchanges are established in Jamaica, Trinidad and Tobago and Barbados to control the trading in shares of public companies. In the main, however, trading in shares is handled by banks and other financial institutions and by lawyers rather than by stock-brokers.

Inspections and Investigations

Regional statutes all include some provisions for the appointment of inspectors to investigate company affairs. The power to appoint is usually vested in the relevant minister or the governor or in the court. It may be exercised on application being made by a prescribed number of shareholders (200 in Jamaica). The applicants must provide evidence establishing a good reason for the appointment to be made by the appointing body who has a discretion in the matter.

To assist an inspector's investigation he is normally given powers to require interested persons to appear before him for examination regarding the affairs of the company and also to produce books of the company. Failure to do so would render the persons liable to penalties.

Particular Territories

• BELIZE (sections 108-110)

Under section 108, in the case of a company having a share capital other than a banking company, on the application of members holding one-tenth of the shares issued, the *court* may appoint inspectors to investigate the affairs of a company and to make a report thereon.

The applicants must show good reason for requiring the investigation and the court may require the applicants to give security for payment of the costs of the enquiry.

It is the duty of all officers and agents of the company to produce to the inspectors all books and documents in their custody or power.

On conclusion of the investigation, the inspectors must submit a report to the court. The registrar of the court must send a copy of the report to the registered office of the company and on request, must send a copy to the applicants.

Under section 109 a company may by special resolution appoint inspectors to investigate its affairs. The inspectors appointed have the same powers as if appointed by the court.

• GUYANA

(a) Cap 89:01 (sections 118 - 120) (existing provisions) Similar provisions as Belize.

(b) Companies Act 1991 (29/1991) (see ss 495 - 514) Under these provisions, powers are given to the Minister, the Court and the Registrar to make inspections and investigations of the affairs of a company. *(N.B.: These provisions are not in effect.)*

• TRINIDAD and TOBAGO (sections 133 - 135)

Similar provisions as in Belize legislation.

• JAMAICA (Companies Act 1965 sections 157-168)

Powers given to Minister and the Court to appoint inspectors to inspect and investigate the affairs of a company and to report thereon on application being made as provided in those sections.

• BARBADOS (sections 420 - 425)

Under section 420, a shareholder of a company or the Registrar may apply to the court for an order that an investigation be made of a company and any of its affiliated companies. An inspector may be appointed for this purpose and his powers will be set out in the order. The inspector must send a copy of his report to the Registrar.

• BAHAMAS (Companies Act 1992 section 280)

Under section 280 the Registrar if he has reasonable cause to suspect that the affairs of a company are being conducted in a fraudulent manner, may, after consultation with the Minister, make a preliminary investigation into the company and submit his findings to the court with a view to the company being wound up and the court may proceed to deal with the company accordingly.

INDEX

Accounts, 182-200
    groups, 195-199, modern accounting
    practice, 183
Action, 154-156
    derivative, 155-156; personal, 155;
    representative, 155
Administration and supervision, 236-238
Amalgamations, 210-211
Annual returns, 123
    specimen form, 124-125
Arrangements, 212
Articles of Association, 24, 49-71
    alteration of, 50-53, 54
    bona fide for the benefit of the
    company, 51; legal effect of, 53-54;
    Table A, 54-71
Audit, 188
Auditors, 182-187

Borrowing, 38-39, 107-112

Capital, 81
    alteration of, 83-84; equity share, 85;
    issued, 82; loan, 81; maintenance of,
    100-106; meaning of, 81; 107-112;
    nominal (or authorized), 82; paid up,
    82, 94; raising of, 81-98; reduction of,
    103-104; reserve, 83; share, 81-82;
    types of, 82-83; uncalled, 83;
Capital reserves, 94
Capitalization issues, 119
CARICOM Report, 1, 6-8, 41-42, 85, 106
Certificate of incorporation, 39
Charges, 109-112
    fixed, 109; floating, 110; register of,
    111; registration of, 111-112
Class rights, 94-95
Co-directors, 177
Committee of inspection, 227
Company, formation of, 21-22;
    promotion of, 72-77; private, 22-24;
    public, 22-24. *See also* Registered
    company, characteristics of
Competing directorates, 177

Compromises, 212
Constructive notice doctrine, 40-41
Contract pre-incorporation, 74-75
Corporate personality, 14
    civil liability, 18, 19-20; criminal
    liability, 18; lifting the veil, 15-17;
    separate personality, 14

Debentures, 108-109
Declaration of compliance, 38
Derivative action, 155-156
Directors, 157
    agents, 164; appointments, 160;
    committee, 173; contracts of,
    170-171; duties of, 169-170;
    managing, 172-173; powers of,
    158-160; register of, 162-163;
    remuneration of, 162; vacation of
    office of, 162
Dissolution, 229
Dividends, 116-120
    assets for, 117-118
Documents for incorporation, 24-25

Equity share capital, 85
Expropriation, 150-152
External companies, 231-235

Foss v Harbottle rule, 5, 146-150
Fraud on minority, 150-151

Historical background, 2-6;
    in the Caribbean Region, 5-6

Incorporation, 21-30
    certificate of, 26-27, 30; documents
    for, 24-25; lifting the veil of, 15-17;
    methods of, 25-27
Insider dealing or trading, 216-218
Internal management rule, 90
Investigation, 153-154

Just and equitable, 152

Legal personality, 14-15
Liability, limited, 17, 42
Liquidation. *See* winding-up
Liquidator, 224, 228
Loan capital, 107-112

Majority rule, 146
Management of company, 163
Manager, 113-115
Managing director, 178
Meetings, 128-143
    general, 129
Membership, 121-127
Memorandum of Association, 24, 32-47
    alternation of, 43-44; example of,
    44-47
Mergers, 210-211
Minority protection, 145, 152

Name, 33-34
    change of, 34; publication, 34

Objects, 35-36, 37-38
Official receiver, 237
Oppressive conduct, 159
Overseas company. *See* External
    companies

Partnership, 10-11, 12-13
Prospectus, 104
Perpetual succession, 18
Poll. *See* Voting
Powers of management, 164
Pre-exemption rights, 103
Preferential shares
Pre-incorporation contracts, 87
Private company, 22-24
    conversion of,23-24
Proceedings, 154
Promoters, duties of, 73-74; expenses,
    76-77; *See also* Company,
    promotion of
prospectus, 104
Proxy, 138
    specimen form of, 143
Public companies, 22-24

Receiver, 113-115
Reconstruction, 211
Register of charges, 35

Register of debenture holders, 35
Register of directors and secretary, 35
Register of directors' interests, 35
Register of members, 35, 121-122
Registered company, 12-13;
    characteristics of, 14-20
Registered office, 34-35
Registrar of Companies, 236
Registration formalities, 25-26
Report on harmonisation of company
    law. *See CARICOM Report*
Representative action, 161
Reserve fund, 120
Resolutions, 134-136
    filing of, 140

Secretary of company, 180
Separate legal personality, 28
Share capital, 42, 92, 81-82;
    alteration, 83
Share certificates, 95-96
Share premium account, 105
Shares, 85-90
    allotment of, 90; classes of, 86-87;
    issue of, 89-90; issued at discount,
    104; par value,84; redeemable, 88,
    104-105; transfer of, 96-98
Sole trader, 24
Statutory declaration of compliance, 258
Stock exchange, 92

Table A, specimen, 67 – 84. *See* Articles
    of Association
Take-over, 213
Transfer of shares, 96-98
Turquand's Case, 78-80

Ultra vires doctrine, 36-37
Unanimous assent, 148

Veil of incorporation, 15-17
Voting, 136-138

Winding up, 219
    compulsory, 220; just and equitable
    ground, 221; voluntary, 225;
    members', 226; creditors', 226